WE ARE EAGLES

INSPIRING STORIES OF IMMIGRANT WOMEN
WHO TOOK BOLD STEPS IN LIFE THROUGH LITERACY

Anna Marie Kukec Tomczyk

WE ARE EAGLES

Cover Design & Layout by Juan Pablo Ruiz
Printed in the United States of America

For more information, contact:
Fig Factor Media, LLC. | www.figfactormedia.com
Anna Marie Kukec Tomczyk | https://amkukectomczyk.com/

ISBN: 978-1-952779-55-8
Library of Congress Number: 2021903860

"THEY THAT HOPE
IN THE LORD WILL
RENEW THEIR
STRENGTH,
THEY WILL SOAR ON
EAGLES' WINGS; THEY
WILL RUN AND NOT
GROW WEARY,
WALK AND NOT GROW
FAINT."

Isaiah 40:31
New American Bible, Revised Edition

TABLE OF CONTENTS

FOREWORD

The Dominican Literacy Center in Aurora, Illinois, began in a small space in a church basement with one rickety card table and two solid folding chairs with one woman who wanted to learn how to read, write and speak English, and one woman who wanted to help her. From that simple beginning, the Dominican Literacy Center evolved into what it is today — a bustling learning community filled with immigrant women and their tutors who meet every week to teach and to learn the baffling language of American English.

After consulting with social workers, counselors and pastors, I soon learned that the most underserved segment in the Aurora area was immigrant women. Aurora is the second largest city in Illinois, second only to Chicago, and 42 percent of the residents are foreign born, according to the U.S. Census. Women who come to Aurora from other countries usually begin working immediately, marry and start their families early, and have no time for English as a Second Language (ESL) classes. Many of them had little or no schooling in their home countries. The Dominican Literacy Center is for those women.

While working to open the center, I also learned another startling statistic: Children whose parents have low literacy levels have a 72% chance of being at the lowest reading levels themselves. These children are more likely to get poor grades, display behavioral problems, have high absentee rates and repeat school years or drop out, according to ProLiteracy (National Bureau of Economic Research, NBER). Beginning an ESL literacy center in Aurora to help women would definitely help not just the women, but their children and families as well.

Over the past 25 years, we have had more than 400 faithful volunteer tutors who have empowered their students to become confident, supported women who read, write and speak English and who are able to lovingly guide their families into life in their new country. Almost 3,000 families now have a mother, an aunt, a grandmother, a sister or a cousin who can read, write and speak English. And all of our immigrant women have had the benefit of learning about life in the United States from their tutors, an adult American woman who often becomes their first American friend.

The Dominican Literacy Center has grown. We now have a large building with conversation classes and U.S. citizenship classes for men and women. These classes include learners from 15 different countries. But the core of the program is still one woman who wants to learn English, and one woman who wants to help her. As Margaret Meade said (lightly edited): "Never doubt that a small group of thoughtful, committed women can change the world. Indeed, they are the only ones who ever have."

From the very beginning of this wonderful program, I could see the "pillars" of Dominican life shining in a new way. Those pillars, which undergird our lives as Dominican women, are community, ministry, study and prayer. Those pillars have always infused my life, but I could see how – in a totally new and unique way – the pillars were supporting our immigrant women as well.

Please enjoy and learn deeply from reading these true stories about the lives of our immigrant women. Their struggles and courage have helped them to become new, literate and informed citizens. We are fortunate to have them in our country, and we are fortunate to be able to partner with them in their new life.

—**Sister Kathleen Ryan, O.P.**
Administrator, Dominican Literacy Center
Aurora, Illinois

* * *

I began practicing law in Aurora, Illinois, in 1982. Since that time, one of my interests has been the representation of immigrants, whether documented or not. In one way, this had to do with my experience in working for the U.S. Immigration and Naturalization Service beginning in 1973 on the Canadian border and elsewhere. In another, after becoming a night law school student and then a lawyer, the reality was to help others less fortunate: an oath taken when given the privilege of being a lawyer in the state of Illinois. This representation was before immigration laws became the topic of the press and politicians today. This work included those who were prospective teachers, families, small business owners and others, who found themselves in removal proceedings. It was not popular.

Aurora enjoys a rich history of various immigrants arriving throughout Kane County. When my grandmother attended St. Nicholas School on High Street, German was spoken. Later, Luxembourg natives, Hungarians and Romanians came and thrived, all seeking refuge in our churches and communities on the near East Side of the Fox River. The school was later renamed Archbishop Oscar Romero School, where the patois was Spanish. It closed a few years ago.

After the Immigration Reform and Control Act (IRCA) was enacted, Aurora had a federal processing office. It was the only one outside Chicago. William Hart, a federal District Court judge and now a former Aurora resident, used to convene citizenship ceremonies at West Aurora High School, the Illinois Math and Science Academy and the Aurora City Hall with the help of a special lady, Linda Barber, from Trinity Episcopal Church. Bill and Kay Hart were our neighbors.

One constant theme or thread, which has underlain all of

these immigrant groups in their quest to become permanent resident aliens and later United States citizens, has been a desire to speak and understand the English language. English language proficiency and knowledge of U.S. history and government are civics requirements to obtain U.S. citizenship. More importantly, English language proficiency has permitted all of these immigrants to become part of American society in their jobs, professions, schools and day-to-day lives. Even in the Immigration and Reform and Control Act of 1986, which now is colloquially referred to as "amnesty," English language proficiency was a centerpiece of federal policy. It was an important attribute for my grandmother, Mae Waegner.

Various groups, including Waubonsee Community College, Trinity Episcopal Church, Centro Cristo Rey and the Dominican Literacy Center, among others, responded to the need to provide English language services to our immigrant community. All of them recognized that Article 10 of our 1970 Illinois Constitution had a fundamental goal, which is to not only promote but to ensure the educational development of all persons to the limit of their capacities. Illinois public schools have taken up this mantle, regardless of whether a person is documented or undocumented.

As a community, we are fortunate to have the women and men who taught English as a second language to those who needed to understand it. My father did so as a retired Illinois government official.

In Plyler v. Doe (1982) 457 U.S. 202, the U.S. Supreme Court held that a Texas statute, which withheld state funds for the education of children who were not "legally admitted" into the United States, and more importantly, denied them enrollment, violated the Equal Protection Clause of the Fourteenth Amendment.

The court held over 35 years ago that: "Public education has a pivotal role in maintaining the fabric of our society, and in sustaining our political and cultural heritage; the deprivation of education takes an inestimable toll in the social, economic, intellectual and psychological well-being of the individual and poses an obstacle to individual achievement: The court considered these concerns in holding the accident of the location of a child's birth did not deprive them of a public education when residing within the jurisdiction of the United States." Frankly, this perspective was a watershed in American jurisprudence. It was not a unanimous opinion. Notwithstanding, it is a hallmark.

A lot of the trials and tribulations of being an immigrant in Aurora have been forgotten. Perhaps, that is as it should be, within the angst of history. But let us pause on the 25th anniversary of the Dominican Literacy Center. Yes, let us celebrate those women and men who served just to serve and their contribution to those who needed it the most. So, as our U.S. Supreme Court correctly stated, they are the fabric of our community. These teachers in Aurora and elsewhere nationwide, were the weavers who made the tapestry of what our country is today.

The book, which follows, is a testament to what they were able to achieve to make our community singular and stronger. I know all of their pupils thank them unequivocally, as should we all.

—Patrick M. Kinnally

Partner, Kinnally Flaherty Krentz Loran Hodge & Masur
Aurora, Illinois

AUTHOR'S NOTE

Growing up on the South Side of Chicago, I learned to appreciate the richness of different neighborhoods with myriad ethnic, racial and religious groups. It made me a part of the larger world. Many of us sought to learn from each other, especially regarding our everyday struggles and our paths to the future.

We also sought the basics: love, comfort, communication, dreams, goodness and safety. While it isn't always possible for some, many of us still strive toward that common foundation. It is all part of the language of life.

I witnessed much of that through the eyes of the immigrants who studied at the Dominican Literacy Centers in Aurora and Melrose Park, Illinois, led by the Dominican Sisters of Springfield, Illinois. They welcomed the world within their doors.

As a former Dominican Associate, I stayed in touch over the years with some Dominican Sisters, including Sister Beth Murphy, who suggested the idea for this book in 2017. She then led me to Sister Kathleen Ryan and Sister Judith Curran, who then led me to Sister Ann Clennon and Sister Beverly Jeanne Howe. I realized that our worlds were smaller than we thought. Through our conversations, I learned that Sister Beverly was the daughter of the late Betty Howe, who was a Dominican Associate with me in the 1990s and we often drove together to meetings with our mentor, the late Sister Mary Ventura.

Since that time, I focused on a journalism career, took care of my dad until he passed away and got married. During those same years, these Dominican Sisters continued to share their knowledge, expertise and time with students, and eventually, with immigrants who crossed their thresholds and sought to improve their lives in some way. They took the initiative to enter their doors, just as they took the brave steps to start anew in the United States. These immigrants then committed to a better future by learning and accepting those changes, both with their families and their communities. The heart of this book then became possible because some of those former students decided to open their hearts and bare their souls, regardless of their trials and triumphs.

Maribel Molina Cortes, Juanita Rodriguez, Maria Dominguez, Blanca Aguilera and Teresa Trenado are the eagles of this book. They each, in their own ways, were stronger than they realized when they decided to leave their nests. They each made a new life in a foreign country and recognized that they needed to change further in order to acclimate to their adopted homes. They tackled goal after goal for themselves and for those they love. The journey for four of these women led to U.S. citizenship, while another started on that path.

I am glad that these women shared what they felt were the most important parts of their lives. I spent about two years listening to them talk as we sat together at their homes, at the literacy center, at a restaurant or even at their local libraries. They smiled. They cried. Some faced physical abuse, poverty and illiteracy, yet they found their inner strength, settled into new homes, learned a new language, earned a living and raised their families. They then tackled milestones that many of us take for granted, and they did so at a later age and with fewer advantages than most. Some of those milestones included learning to drive a car and getting a driver's license; landing jobs and promotions; and saving enough money to buy their first homes. They also felt a special sense of pride when they witnessed their children become the first in their families to graduate high school or college.

Moments like these led to We Are Eagles, a book that offers inspiring, true stories about the founding and first 25 years of the Dominican Literacy Center as told through the eyes of these immigrant women and how their lives changed after they passed through the doors of this center.

These women, who also represent countless others, are the eagles who found their path, became empowered and, eventually, soared above the clouds. Their accomplishments follow the most basic, everyday things to more complex, dramatic events that offer relatable points for just about anyone. And since each one of these women attended the Dominican Literacy Center in Aurora at different times, and their lives took separate paths, their hearts all led back to the center. Many former students also reunited during a 25th anniversary celebration at the center in Aurora, marking yet another milestone for both the center's enduring mission and the adult students it helped to guide.

The women in this book all had one thing in common: the arc of their lives paralleled each other, regardless of the year they attended the center. This book, therefore, starts with the first public speech by Maribel that heralds more accomplishments to come. Then their stories are divided into four parts that mark the lifecycle of the eagle, one of the most powerful and enduring birds in our country. They are:

Part 1: Life in the Nest focuses on their lives before leaving the long-time environments that they each knew, whether it was their homes in Mexico, a marriage in the United States or even the standard classroom.

Part 2: Leaving the Nest shows how each woman transitions from their long-time environments in order to set the foundations that would lead to their goals and achievements.

Part 3: Choosing to Fly follows each woman as they decide to change their lives even further and how they learned to adapt to their new experiences.

Part 4: Soaring Above the Clouds shows the results of their earlier decisions and how they found new freedom to live, to love and to be accepted as strong, independent women who succeeded with their families, their communities, jobs and other goals.

Also, the title of this book came from Maribel's daughter. She gleefully announced that since her mother learned to drive and now had a car, the two of them were like eagles who could fly anywhere. Nothing could hold them back. Indeed, nothing held back Maribel or the others as they gained strength, confidence and endurance for their journey in life.

That is why I hope others will be inspired by these stories to achieve their own goals or advance their education in some way, which could help them to strengthen their wings for a new future. I also hope this book encourages others to see the immense value in literacy and to be generous in their thoughts, words and deeds by supporting the Dominican Literacy Centers and all such educators nationwide.

Together, we have a vested interest in this mission to keep all such eagles in flight.

—Anna Marie Kukec Tomczyk
Owner, Forest Glen Media LLC
Chicago, Illinois

PROLOGUE:
MARIBEL'S GRADUATION SPEECH

Maribel Molina Cortes placed her prepared speech on the podium and faced an audience for the first time in her life. While she was nervous, she also was proud to be chosen to speak at the English as a Second Language Recognition Ceremony where many of them were receiving Certificates of Achievement at Waubonsee Community College in Aurora, Illinois, the same city she arrived in so long ago from her native Mexico.

This day was special for many reasons, but especially because two women expectedly arrived and were sitting in the audience. Maribel now wanted to wholeheartedly acknowledge them and began her speech.

I want to thank everyone for being here today. I especially want to thank all of my classmates, who chose me to represent them on behalf of the English as a Second Language (ESL) Class of 2009.

The reason why I am here is because I was a victim of domestic violence and I want to prove to you that dreams do come true.

I started taking English classes because of my daughter. I remember one night, my little girl wanted me to read to her from a book that had the picture of a dog on the cover. Well, I could not read the book. I did not know how to read English. But since the book had a picture of a dog on the cover, I just made up a story about a dog. She was pleased and she then went to sleep.

Well, the next night, she grabbed the same book and asked me to read it again. This time, I forgot the story that I told her the night before and I just made up another one. She said, 'You are a liar, mommy!' I was shocked and asked her why she said that to me. She then said, 'You said something different yesterday!'

I felt very bad because I could not even read a little book to my daughter. I also could not even help her with her homework. That's when I realized how important the English language was in our lives.

So, everything I learned about the English language began when I met Sister Kathleen Ryan and Sister Ann Clennon at the Dominican Literacy Center. I was a domestic violence survivor when I met them and I was going through a divorce, and they were my first English teachers in this country. I remember that every single time we met for class, they always had hot coffee on a winter day or a cup of soup on a rainy day. They were always there to help me. They became more than my teachers. They were my angels. And thanks to the kindness and the love they had for us, that helped me to continue with my life and to always do better.

When I finished their program at the center, they recommended that I take extra classes at Waubonsee Community College. They said that if I continued to study English, it would help me to make a better life for myself and for my daughter. So, I was grateful to graduate from the center and to now graduate from Waubonsee. I will continue to have a better life because of it.

I just want to say thank you and to let you all know that dreams do come true, especially if you work hard and believe in yourself. Also, God always sends angels to your life. For me, Sister Kathleen and Sister Ann were my angels.

PART 1
LIFE IN THE NEST

Chapter 1

MARIBEL SURVIVES AN ABUSIVE MARRIAGE

In 1992, Maribel left Tlaxcala, just east of Mexico City, with her 4-year-old daughter, Mary, because it was her duty to be with her husband as he looked for work in the Chicago area. She was committed to keeping their marriage together in the United States, a country where she believed that the American dream was possible.

She also was eager to celebrate Christmas in this country. The streets of Aurora, about 40 miles southwest of Chicago, were fluffed with freshly fallen snow that gently formed pillows on top of the holiday lights. The scene at dusk was magical and Maribel deluded herself into thinking that same magic could somehow change her marriage.

But that holiday magic soon faded. The three of them began living with friends to save money and her husband insisted that Maribel stay indoors 24 hours a day to take care of Mary. He said it was for her own safety in a strange country. So, she kept telling herself that such confinement was supposed to be normal, but then wondered about the freedom the United States was supposed to offer.

Soon, her husband was coming home later and later and acting strangely. He also began hitting her so hard that, one night, the neighbors on the first floor came to see if everything was OK. He threatened that if she opened the door to anyone, they would be taken away because they were illegals. Instead, her husband kept the door closed, so no one would see Maribel's wounds. He told the concerned neighbors that Maribel fell and hurt herself and she was all right now.

The neighbors hesitated and asked Maribel directly through the door if she was OK and said they planned to call the police if she did not answer. Her husband held Maribel's hair tightly, nearly pulling out the roots. He then shoved her to answer.

"I'm fine, thank you," Maribel answered with a strained voice.

What Maribel thought was the American dream continued to dissolve with each of his verbal jabs that led to his repeated kicks to her face. Her blood splattered the walls. Her nose was broken. Her eyes were blackened.

The beatings continued along with the threats. He warned

that if she left him, her family would suffer the consequences. He threatened to burn down her mother's home. Or he would pay a friend to rape her younger sister. Or he would get someone to beat up her brother. Each threat shook Maribel to her core.

So, she remained silent. She buried the pain deep inside and never told her family that this nightmare had replaced her American dream.

One day, Maribel learned about her husband's affairs and summoned the courage to finally confront him. It just led to more beatings. He then accused Maribel of being unfaithful. It continued until she cried and bled more. Her husband later claimed the money he earned was not enough to feed them, so he needed to be away most of the time. When her purse was empty, Maribel resorted to borrowing money from his relatives just to buy food.

Then one day, Maribel came across a magazine article about domestic abuse. She then hid the magazine and only read it when her husband was away. The article advised women to store clothes, important documents and some money in a hiding place in case of an emergency. Maribel then packed some clothes for both her and Mary and hid them. She stopped asking her husband anything and was almost relieved that he was gone nearly every day and night. Her heart began to race just thinking of her escape. Then she froze. If she did leave him ... would he find her? Would he become so enraged that he would literally beat her to death? What then would happen to Mary?

One night when Maribel was sleeping, Mary crept under the covers and cuddled with her in the bed. Her husband unexpectedly came home late and sucker punched the sleeping Maribel in the face. Little Mary woke up in sheer terror and raced from the bedroom. Maribel felt one powerful blow after another, coming in rapid succession. When the punches subsided, Maribel was forced to sleep with her husband.

The next morning, Maribel's nose and mouth were so swollen that her left eye was fully closed and her right eye was red. Maribel looked into a mirror on the wall and searched for her face. It wasn't her staring back.

She cried for being too cowardly to defend herself, too weak to fight back and not smart enough to do something about it. Maribel saw no other way out and contemplated slitting her wrists. She even set aside which kitchen knife to use. Before she would end it all, she needed to take one last look at her daughter, who was sleeping in bed with the moonlight covering her sweet, small face.

For just a moment, Maribel felt a sense of peace while looking at a part of herself that would carry on in the world. Just then, Mary unexpectedly woke up crying and asked her mother to never abandon her. Did Mary somehow know what Maribel was about to do? After all, her little Mary was mature beyond her years and always looked out for her. That's when Maribel decided to put the knife away.

Then during their last struggle, her husband's hands locked around Maribel's neck. She felt, strangely, that this could be a swift solution to all the problems that he said were her fault. But she could not die. Not now. Her daughter deserved a better life.

After years of beatings so progressively worse and living with the constant fear he would kill her, Maribel discarded her strong religious commitment to marriage, grabbed her emergency bag of clothes and escaped with Mary. She then got an order of protection against her husband in a legal system she knew little about and did not know the language.

Chapter 2

JUANITA FACES POVERTY AND DANGER

Juanita Rodriguez, who was raised in the small town of Guanajuato in central Mexico, was the youngest of nine sisters, where each one always needed to find their own place, whether it was in line for dinner or a warm spot in bed. They all helped their father, Jose Rodriguez, as he took care of their cows, horses, chickens, pigs and roosters, along with a few dogs and cats, on the land they rented. Some of the animals fed their family. Most, though, were sold for much-needed cash.

As a child, Juanita did not attend school. Her father didn't believe it was necessary. Instead, at 5 years old, she began helping her mother, Luz Lopez, with chores around their small, one-room adobe house. Everyone slept, ate or dressed in that one room. Their privacy was thinly veiled by curtains that divided the space. While they could not see beyond those curtains, every word or snore or giggle was heard. Juanita got used to it as she slept with three of her sisters in a full-size bed. There was no indoor plumbing. So, when they needed to use the toilet, they went outside.

Without any running water inside their home, Juanita had to wash clothes in a nearby creek. She also carried a heavy clay pot on one shoulder or on top of her head, while laboriously carrying the water between the creek and the house. The heavy weight of the clay pot with the water was tiring, but she knew it was necessary to help her family. The creek squeezed to a trickle during the dry season from September through January. That's when Juanita walked further to a well, where she pulled a rope attached to a bucket that lifted the water up from the darkness below. She toted enough water each day for her family and carried even more jars back to water the animals. If the animals died due to the lack of water, they all could die, too. Their lives depended on each other.

The floor inside their home was dirt, just like the roads outside. No concrete sidewalks or streets or platforms. Her father built the house behind a stone fence, which offered protection from the elements and the few vehicles that happened to pass. But the fence and house often needed repairs, which kept her father busy. While the chickens freely roamed around outside, they were just as free inside the house, especially when the weather turned cold.

Juanita's day often started around 5 a.m. as she fed the chickens, then the cows and horses. Later, she helped her mother make tortillas to help feed the family. If she wasn't outside, she stayed inside and used the daylight as it streamed into their small home, so she could prepare different foods by hand, helping her mother every day as they cooked together. Her work continued until nighttime, and even then, they lit candles and oil lamps until they finished their chores.

Work was second nature to Juanita, because she felt it was important to always help her family. She wanted to take care of them since they all worked long hours on the farm. At least they had some money for necessities. But they had little food and often no shoes, mostly because they grew out of them so quickly. Without shoes, Juanita often found herself stepping on a rock or cow manure while trying to get around the animals. When it stormed, Juanita stood in mud and grabbed onto the nearest tree to keep the strong winds from blowing her away. She held on tightly, a grip much stronger than expected from such a small, thin girl. That type of strength, when she most needed it, made her feel stronger than the wind. And she knew that once she grew up, nothing would blow her down.

***

Over the years, Juanita stayed home while her sisters eventually moved to the United States. They found jobs and often sent money to their parents. Juanita felt compelled to do the same, eager to show her family that she could contribute just as much. When Juanita decided to leave home, she moved to Moroleón, Guanajuato, Mexico, which had small factories that made and sold clothing directly to people.

She walked into one of the factories and asked for a job as a seamstress. They didn't ask about her experience. But they did want her to show how she could make a blouse. She sat down at a sewing machine, assembled some material and quickly made a blouse. The supervisor was so impressed, he immediately hired her. That's when she started sewing more blouses, along with dresses and pants. Her shift was from 9 a.m. until 8 p.m., Mondays through Saturdays, with only a break for lunch. The constant hum of the sewing machine, and her desire to earn more money, quickly led her to becoming efficient with her time. After all, every minute meant more money, since she was paid for each piece that was completed. Her diligence soon allowed her to start saving money for herself, while still being able to send money back home to her parents.

Juanita stayed at the sewing factory for about four years, perfecting her work techniques, earning and saving more money, and learning to live on her own. But when the woman who owned the factory died, the business was sold. After the new owners took over, the operations were not the same. So, Juanita decided to look for another job and, eventually, found a position selling shoes at a store in town.

While the change in jobs was welcome, something else was not. She noticed four young men began to watch her commute each day between her home and the store. Juanita realized that as she matured and learned new skills in the factory and the store, it allowed her to live independently, like other young women. But that new-found freedom was attracting the wrong kind of attention for many young women at the time. Now, she sensed that for herself. Although she kept to herself, she noticed that the same four men who appeared to be friends, would track her every move — when she left in the morning and when she returned home at night.

Sometimes, they openly followed her. Whenever she spotted them, chills raced up her spine. She didn't want trouble and she feared the worse. Would they attack her? Would they rob her of her savings, or worse?

Every day, she kept her distance and they did, too. But they were obviously trailing her every move and she realized she could face the same fate as other women her age. Such men often kidnapped and raped women or forced them into marriage. She was sure they would give her no choice and she wanted nothing to do with any of that. So, she went to the police and filed a report. But the police did nothing.

Then one night, one of the men approached her. He moved so close that Juanita trembled, fearing he would do something right there.

"I want you," he whispered.

Juanita tried to hide her fear and ignored him as she quickened her step, hoping to get home safely.

"I will marry you or rape you," he told her. "You have to pick one."

At 19, Juanita's fear was realized. She was his target. She was nothing more than a conquest that would cost her greatly. She then ran away from him. Once home, she barricaded the door. She did not want any of them, let alone the one who threatened to rape her. She just wanted to be able to earn a living and to help her family, not face threats against her life, her body and her dignity. And what if she were raped and became pregnant, how would she raise a baby on her own? Her fears continued to multiply.

Whenever she wanted to leave the house, she was forced to look out the windows to see who was hanging around. If she saw any of those men nearby, she stayed home. She often hesitated to go outside for fear of running into them again ... or worse.

Chapter 3

BLANCA FUELS HER FUTURE

Blanca Gonzales Aguilera was born and raised in Marin, Mexico, the fourth in line with a sister and three brothers. She often helped with family chores, including cooking, cleaning and using a scrub board to wash clothes. Afterwards, she relaxed by crocheting, like her mother Maria Gonzales, who created handmade sweaters and other items for the family. Blanca's mother was a good cook and Blanca learned much just by watching her. She also helped by cutting and preparing the fruits and vegetables, while her mother easily made different dishes throughout the day.

Sometimes, Blanca was tempted to scoop up and discard the grease that collected at the top of simmering soups and stews. But her mother tapped her hand away, wanting to keep everything in the pot.

"No. That is all the taste," her mother said.

Blanca also enjoyed baking cookies nearly every day. They loved to eat the cookies with coffee during the mid-afternoon merienda, or snack. While lunch was their heaviest meal of the day with hearty soups or beans, the dinner later in the evening was often lighter and, sometimes, included eggs.

Her father, Alcibiades Gonzales, played guitar and sang at local events, including weddings, parties and festivals. He loved music and, even more, he loved making his living at it. Then, he decided to cross the border into the United States to get more work to support his growing family. He worked as a janitor at an airport and then as a packer at Brach's candy factory in Chicago. Every nine or ten months, he would return to his family in Mexico, stayed for a while and then headed back to work in the United States.

Her family was humble and loving, and they lived in a three-bedroom home that offered a kitchen, TV room and ample closets. But due to their limited income, Blanca stopped attending school in the sixth grade. That's when Blanca stepped into the workforce in Mexico, aiming to earn enough money to help her parents and siblings. What work could she do?

She was eager to start her own sewing business.

That's when she began to ride the bus to take sewing classes, where she learned to use a sewing machine and follow patterns to make blouses and dresses. When she finished the course, she earned a certificate that she proudly shared with her family. She then took the initiative to start her sewing business and soon became known around the area for her quality work in making various types of clothes for men and women, as well as a new black cassock for a priest.

Besides her love for her family and for sewing, Blanca also was dedicated to her faith. She loved her long-time Catholic church, Parroquia de Nuestra Señora de la Asunción de Marin. The building was made of bone-colored stucco with a stately bell tower, all surrounded by a wrought-iron fence atop a concrete foundation. Near the church were a plaza and gazebo, where many people often met and walked around, especially on Sundays when most enjoyed a beautiful day socializing with friends or watching their children play on the lush green grass and trees. The church meant a lot to Blanca because it represented the strength of her faith and the power of her prayer.

Besides worshiping there, she spent about five years singing in the church choir and taught first-grade catechism, so the next generation would know Jesus just as she did. Prayer came naturally to her and she sang some of those prayers each week in the choir at the Sunday Masses.

Chapter 4

TERESA SOWS AN UNEXPECTED PATH

Teresa Soto Trenado lacked a full education because her primary job was to work in the fields near her home in Guanajuato, in central Mexico. Since she was 7 years old, she used her small hands to plant corn, beans and other vegetables by following her father, Ignacio Soto, as he led a team of two horses that plowed the fields.

Strapped around her waist was a cloth sack made by her mother, Elena Trejo, and it bulged with a supply of seeds for the field. Teresa dug her small hand inside the sack and pulled out a fistful of the seeds, knowing that soon they would start poking through the soil.

As the horses dragged a plow to open a row, Teresa followed by stepping forward with one leg, planting a seed, then stepping forward with her other leg and planting another seed. Her gait allowed for just enough space between the seeds to allow the plants to grow unencumbered in the field. She did this throughout the daylight hours. When the field was fully seeded, the horses were given time to rest.

On some days, Teresa got up around 7 a.m. in their brown brick home, which had a small kitchen and two bedrooms, all shared with her nine sisters and two brothers. Teresa walked every day to school, which took about three hours. The Lerma River, which runs from the Mexican Plateau to Lake Chapala, near Guadalajara, Jalisco, often determined if Teresa went to school or not. If a heavy rain swelled the river to overflowing, then she couldn't cross it by foot to get to school. Otherwise, she went to school every day, until she finished the fifth grade.

When it was time for feeding the animals, Teresa used a spreader that she filled with feed and then bent over, low to the ground, and cranked the handle. The spreader then sprayed out seeds in a fan-like motion, as if waving to the land. The cows would come and bend their heads just enough so their thick tongues could lap up the seeds. The back-breaking drudgery of farm life was difficult as they all worked in the fields. It was enough to make Teresa want to escape.

At age 15, she did.

***

Teresa caught the eye of 21-year-old Miguel, who was paid by Teresa's parents as a farm hand. They often talked whenever he had a free moment away from harvesting the crops that she initially planted. But their moments together were often in secret.

Then in 1983, Ignacio found Teresa talking with Miguel and tore her away. Fear raced through Teresa as she saw how enraged her father was. She watched him slide off his belt, and she knew what was coming. The belt sliced into her flesh, whipping her second after second. The beating was so painful and humiliating, she vowed to escape.

Teresa slipped out at night and went to the home of Miguel's parents, which was a short distance away. Her wounds eventually healed, but her heart did not. So, Teresa stayed with Miguel's family for about two months until they got married.

On their wedding day, Teresa wore a simple, white bridal gown and Miguel wore his only good suit during a traditional church wedding Mass. There was no reception or party afterward. They could not afford it, especially since Miguel was now unemployed.

Eventually, Teresa encouraged Miguel to go to Mexico City to find work. They then moved to Mexico City, near a basilica, and rented a room with a gas stove and a bed.

***

While Teresa gained a husband, she seemingly lost her father. The news of their marriage was hard on Ignacio and he stopped talking to his daughter. Teresa's brothers and sisters often begged their father to reconsider. But he was too proud. He was upset that Miguel did not ask for Teresa's hand in marriage, so no permission was granted. Besides, he firmly believed that Teresa was too young to get married.

After about a year, Teresa continued to be upset by the silence between her and her father. She missed not being included in family events, such as birthdays and holidays. The separation from her family made her heart ache. Her mother also was so upset by the estrangement that she eventually decided to take matters into her own hands. Elena wanted her family back together.

So, when the moment seemed right, Elena asked Ignacio to reunite with Teresa. He finally agreed. That's when Elena quickly arranged a meeting between Ignacio and Teresa at their home.

"Can you come here?" Elena asked Teresa.

"Yes, of course," said Teresa, stunned at the sudden invitation to enter her parents' home again.

When the day arrived, Teresa greeted her mother, who hugged her, but then quickly stepped aside, praying that the reunion would work. Theresa was now entering further inside her old home with caution, not knowing how her father would react when he saw her for the first time in about a year.

When they met face to face, Teresa somehow felt relieved to finally see her father again. He looked at her, then his eyes cast downward in sadness instead of anger. Ignacio was silent and then looked back at his daughter.

"I ... love ... you," Ignacio said haltingly. "But I always felt you were too young to marry."

Ignacio also admitted that he was worried it might set a precedent among her sisters. Teresa finally understood. They apologized to each other. They embraced. It was comforting to once again hear her father's voice talk to her like a daughter.

From that moment forward, Teresa and Miguel celebrated with her family during every birthday and holiday. It felt good to once again enjoy the hugs, the kisses and the return of their warmth.

***

While one chapter in Teresa's life ended, another began in the early morning of September 1985.

The buildings in Mexico City began to shake and dishes and pottery inside homes crashed to the floor. An earthquake snapped homes in half, sending walls and roofs crashing amid massive clouds of dirt and debris ballooning into the air. Teresa's eyes widened and filled with terror. She ran outside into the street, seeking some type of refuge from the falling bricks and glass.

Teresa saw her ravaged Mexico City, with collapsed walls and roofs and windows that seemed to slice into the dustladened air. Her senses collided as screams filled her ears and chaos filled her eyes.

As the earth calmed, Teresa and Miguel were told to stay away from their apartment until the building could be inspected to verify if it was safe to return inside.

Luckily, the earthquake did not seriously damage their building, so they did return. However, more aftershocks continued later, so the fear of more buildings collapsing remained on Teresa's mind as they tenuously tried to resume normal living.

The following year, the city then experienced a series of natural gas explosions that blew some homes to smithereens. Teresa and Miguel lived a few miles away from the explosions, yet they felt them rumble throughout their apartment building. It was enough to cause fear and chaos again among their neighbors. Many people then fled to the mountains for about three days, hoping to wait out any other explosions and falling debris.

Teresa and Miguel also hiked up the mountains to seek refuge. Volunteers soon arrived to provide everyone with blankets, water and food, such as tortas or sandwiches. Teresa then laid the blankets on the ground, where they slept.

The next day, Teresa became nauseated and threw up. Was it the stress of this emergency? The fear of dying? Miguel suggested that Teresa stay with her mother for a few days and she agreed.

After a week, Teresa returned to Miguel at their apartment in Mexico City and told him why she had been so sick.

She was pregnant.

Chapter 5

MARIA FACES PAIN BEFORE LOVE

Maria Dominguez was born and raised in Valle de Juarez in central western Mexico, and her family survived, like many in the region, by growing corn and making cheese from cow's milk. Maria's father, Juan Manuel Contreras, had a few cows, but he did not own the land he managed. Little did Maria realize at the time, that one of her fondest memories of her father would be watching him, sitting on top of his horse, as he checked on his cows and distributed food to them. Years later, when Maria was 33, he was hit by a truck while he was in a roadway and died five days later.

But as a young girl, Maria helped to raise her two brothers and two sisters while they lived together in an adobe house with a tile roof. Their mother, Remedios Torres, helped her husband tend to the farm animals each day. Remedios went out every morning to milk the cows and brought every drop home, so she could make it into cheese.

Maria knew she needed and wanted an education. But her father believed farming would give his family a good life and did not believe that attending school was important. Instead of heading to school each day, Maria as the oldest, took care of her brothers and sisters. She changed their diapers and then washed them in the stream that flowed down from the mountains and made its way past the front of their home. While she bent over the stream, she also occasionally watched other neighbors clean their laundry the same way. They scrubbed stains by rubbing the cloth over a big stone. There was always at least one stone near every home that "belonged" to each family. The water that freely flowed by their home supplied many of their needs. But there was no sewer system in the area and they lacked indoor plumbing. Instead, they carried empty buckets to the stream, filled them with water and brought them inside their home, where the water was used for cooking, cleaning and their personal needs.

Despite tending cows, Maria's father did not make enough money to support all of them and the scarcity of food in the house showed. There also was not much work in the area. As a result, her father would borrow money to use as he crossed the border into the United States and spent a few months at a time working as a landscaper or as a farmer. He saved his wages and later returned home with the money. But Maria cried every time her father returned. She knew that the money he brought would not buy enough food for the family.

Because of the scarcity of food, young Maria was sent more than 300 miles away to live with her Aunt Carmella in Mexico City. At 10 years old, Maria was enlisted as a helper in her aunt's grocery store, where she straightened the merchandise on the shelves, cleaned the floors and retrieved items for customers. She supposedly earned a small wage. But while her aunt promised to send her wages directly to her parents, Maria and her parents never saw any of the money.

All through middle school, Maria worked for Aunt Carmella, but their relationship was strained and they never grew close.

One day, Maria fainted in church and a doctor diagnosed her with anemia. Aunt Carmella said she had no time to cook for Maria in order to help strengthen her. So, another aunt, Angelita, offered to provide dinner to Maria. So, Maria went after school to Aunt Angelita's house, gulped down the meal and rushed back to the grocery store to work.

It was an endless work cycle. Maria also woke up at 5 a.m. each day to clean Aunt Carmella's home and then took a bucket of water and a broom to wash the sidewalks around the home before leaving for school.

During one school break, Maria returned home to visit

with her parents and begged her mother not to send her back to Aunt Carmella's store. Her parents were unconvinced and told Maria to go back anyway.

***

Maria was excited about her upcoming graduation ceremony from sixth grade. One night she had to stay after class so she could be fitted for a graduation gown. But taking the measurements of students in line took longer than expected, and Maria increasingly became anxious. She knew she was going to be late arriving for her shift at the store. Yet, she did not want to leave the line, because she was so close to being fitted to ensure her graduation gown would look good on one of the most important days of her life.

After her measurements were taken, Maria bolted from the school just as it started to rain. She ran through the streets of Mexico City to her aunt's store, hoping her tardiness would not be noticed. Maria quietly slipped into the back door and started to quietly work. Aunt Carmella still noticed Maria was late and told her to leave.

Aunt Carmella then dragged Maria to the door, gripping her hair, and flung her recklessly into the street during the now heavy rainstorm. Aunt Carmella then slammed the door behind her. Maria splash landed into a deep puddle, getting soaked by the muddy water and the driving rain.

Just then, another aunt, Yolanda, happened to find Maria as she was trying cautiously to pick herself up from the muddy water without slipping. Crying, Maria looked up at Yolanda, who asked what happened. Maria tearfully explained how her joyful day turned so sad, and Aunt Yolanda promised to talk with Aunt Carmella.

A few days later, Aunt Yolanda and her husband invited Maria to move in with them and Maria quickly agreed.

Soon afterward, Maria found a job at a camera store in Mexico City and each time she received her wages in her hand, she sent most of them to her parents. Maria also called her parents on occasion because the owner of the camera store generously allowed her to use the store phone for free.

***

As Maria commuted to the camera store each day, she passed a home where a young man named Valentin lived with his family. Valentin occasionally went to the same grocery store where Maria used to work. It was at that store, where Valentin first noticed Maria, who was easy to spot because of her red sweater and her long, beautiful hair that fell to her knees. He liked Maria, but thought it wasn't possible to introduce himself since she avoided talking directly to the customers. So, he hesitated to start any conversations. And when Maria left work at the end of the day, she also noticed Valentin. They looked at each other briefly. But, again, Valentin hesitated to approach her.

Weeks later, Maria ran into Valentin at a neighborhood party and he asked her to dance. She declined because she didn't know how to dance. She also was too shy and awkward, lacking confidence in how she would move in front of a boy. Valentin asked her to dance again and she finally agreed. Her dancing was, indeed, awkward as her thin arms and legs tried to find the beat. Valentin even commented about her dancing. Embarrassed, Maria immediately stopped dancing and left. While their meeting abruptly ended at the party, Maria continued to notice Valentin more as they met at the bus stop and, soon, they started talking again.

Maria eventually decided to return to her hometown and stayed with her parents. That's where she met a boy, who was eager to date her. Maria agreed, but soon learned that he drank a lot. Maria quickly decided that was not the relationship she wanted and returned to Mexico City, where she renewed her friendship with Valentin. They then started to date.

In 1983, after Maria turned 20, she married Valentin. They had a simple civil ceremony in her hometown followed by a small family dinner.

Later, in Mexico City, they married in a Catholic church, where Maria wore a long, white bridal gown. For Maria, her marriage to Valentin finally felt real.

Chapter 6

THE CENTER AND GOD'S WHISPER

On a crisp winter day in February 1993, Sister Kathleen Ryan was drinking coffee in the convent of St. Peter's in Aurora, where she worked as a substitute for a third- and fourth-grade teacher on maternity leave. She turned on the TV and watched the "CBS News Sunday Morning" show with news anchor, Charles Kuralt. One segment of the newsmagazine featured two members of the Sisters of Mercy religious community, who started a literacy program in Bridgeport, Connecticut. They served underprivileged immigrant women seeking to learn how to speak English so they could fit into their new society.

Sister Kathleen, a long-time educator and former principal, listened intently. She was immediately intrigued.

"I would love to do that!" she thought as her slender fingers gently put down the coffee mug.

In some ways, Sister Kathleen felt starting a literacy center would be daunting. She knew very little about the immigrant community from Mexico or other South American countries. She was born and raised on Chicago's Northwest Side, where her middle-class neighbors were Polish, Irish, Scottish and Italian. Many had grandparents living with them. That was how life was.

Still, Sister Kathleen realized that more and more immigrants were coming into the Chicago area. So, a literacy center would help to fill a growing need as immigrants sought to acclimate to their new country. During the early 1990s, about 250,000 legal immigrants lived in Illinois, with even more estimated to be illegal, so totals could be as high as 355,000 around the state. They were mostly from Poland, Mexico, Central America and Asia, especially India and Korea, and they settled around the Chicago region, according to the Center for Immigration Studies and U.S. Census figures.

Sister Kathleen felt the immigration ranks would continue to increase. So, a literacy center would serve a growing base and would become more important than ever for the future of the community. The drive to start a program similar to what the Sisters of Mercy provided in Connecticut motivated her. So, Sister Kathleen quickly started sketching out an initial plan.

By the following week, she gathered Dominican Sisters Virginia Derhake, Mary Harris, Ann Clennon and Judith

Curran, who all lived with her. She knew they would provide great feedback, including how to find the right location, the best way to establish the center and what to include in the curriculum. They acted as a collective sounding board, a way to point her in the right direction, to help fulfill their mission by helping those on the margin of society.

Sister Kathleen listened to them intently, especially Sister Judith. They had known each other since they were students at Notre Dame High School for Girls in Chicago. During those years, Sister Kathleen had an interest in becoming a religious sister, who was more active in the world, compared to nuns, who were cloistered. She and Judith both discovered they were drawn to the Dominican Sisters of Springfield. By age 18 in 1964, Kathleen joined the Dominican Sisters. She also graduated from St. Ambrose University in Davenport, Iowa, and earned a master's degree in educational administration and supervision from St. Thomas University in St. Paul, Minnesota, which helped to prepare her for many of her missions. It also would help her to manage the literacy center.

Sister Kathleen and Sister Judith also worked together periodically over the years, including when Sister Judith became a principal at an elementary school and enlisted Sister Kathleen to replace a lay teacher, who went on maternity leave.

Now, all those year later, Sister Judith listened intently as

Sister Kathleen presented her idea for the literacy center and was enthusiastic. Each of the sisters then encouraged Sister Kathleen to get more information.

After the meeting, Sister Kathleen called CBS-TV to order a video of the eight-minute Charles Kuralt segment. She then called the Sisters of Mercy to talk with the sisters featured in the program, and they in turn, told her about the books they used in the curriculum and the program's format. It gave her a great foundation to build a convincing study to present to her congregation about the need for the new literacy center. Most of all, she believed, the literacy center could help to change lives.

Then, Sister Kathleen planned to speak with Sister Rose Miriam Schulte, the prioress general of their congregation in Springfield, Illinois. The motherhouse on Monroe Street was their anchor, particularly during their transition from Vatican II, which reverberated throughout the Catholic Church. One of the most noticeable changes happened when the Dominican Sisters stopped wearing their long, traditional black-and-white floor-length habits and long flowing veils and they switched to knee-length habits with shorter veils. They also were allowed to expose their bangs just below the tops of their veils. Later, they were offered the opportunity to wear conservative civilian clothing, such as black skirts and white blouses along with a simple cross around their necks.

Besides their living facilities, the motherhouse had a beautiful chapel with stained-glass windows that stretched toward Heaven. The sanctuary was built with wood and Belgian marble and included a stand-alone altar. On the wall behind the altar, was a massive crucifix and statues of St. Catherine of Sienna on the right and St. Dominic on the left. Below the statues was a large mosaic with a grouping of other saints. Sister Kathleen and other sisters would often sing in this chapel, or they sometimes sat in silent prayer. Or they faced other sisters across the main aisle and alternated chants from one side to the other.

The chapel and the motherhouse were at the heart of their prayerful lives and their mission to educate. Now, Sister Kathleen believed the literacy center could become an important educational mission, so it was important to get the approval and blessing of the congregation's leadership. Sister Kathleen aimed to follow the process established in her congregation.

"It fits right in with our congregation's most recent chapter statement, which puts a focus on working with people on the margins," said Sister Rose Miriam. The chapter statement summarized the aspirations and commitments of the religious community made during a periodic governance meeting, called a General Chapter.

"I agree, and there are a lot of immigrant women who need

help, and more are expected to move into the Chicago area in the future," said Sister Kathleen.

After their discussion, Sister Rose Miriam spoke to the leadership team. The sisters then voted on the idea and approved it … on one condition: Sister Kathleen would need to obtain enough funding to totally support the program in one year.

The leadership team then sent Sister Kathleen a letter in the mail, granting her request to spend the next year working on her plan to establish the new literacy center and to seek the necessary funding to keep it viable.

Back in the Chicago area, Sister Kathleen opened a letter from her congregation. As she finished reading it, she saw a check for $10,000. A glint came to her eyes and her enormous smile exposed her joy. The congregation approved the project and provided the seed money to get started on this dream project. More importantly, it was seed money to help immigrant women achieve their own American dreams.

PART 2
LEAVING THE NEST

Chapter 7

MARIBEL STANDS ON THE THRESHOLD

Maribel and Mary were being driven by Christina, a social worker handling Maribel's domestic case. The sun was shining on this mild autumn day in 1995 as they drove up to the red-brick, two-story building near Farnsworth Avenue and Liberty Street in Aurora.

The sidewalk was covered with colorful leaves that crunched beneath their shoes as they walked up four steps and stood on the concrete porch. Maribel noticed the white lace curtains in the windows and on the front door. To the left of the door was a white square sign attached to the wall that had simple black letters: Dominican Literacy Center. The former convent once housed several religious sisters, who taught at the adjacent St. Therese of Jesus Catholic School and served throughout the community. Instead of those religious sisters, the building now was filled with immigrant students. Inside, Maribel was told, were volunteer lay tutors and some Dominican Sisters of Springfield, a Catholic religious order of educators, who were teaching immigrants like her to speak and to understand English.

But Maribel didn't have time for English classes. She was working two shifts that she desperately needed to support herself and her daughter. She just wanted to survive in this country that she knew little about and to avoid her abusive husband. The social worker already helped her a lot during this tough time, and Maribel knew something had to change in her life. So, when the social worker said she had a surprise, Maribel went along with it.

"This is my surprise," the social worker said in Spanish to Maribel after they arrived. "If you want to get a job that's better than cleaning toilets at Marshall Field's, you will need to learn English."

Ay, Dios mío! That would take too long, Maribel thought. She didn't have that kind of time. She was just the daughter of a poor woman, who worked 15-hour days selling fruit at a market near Tlaxcala. What Maribel needed now was a good job that earned more money. She needed to put food on the table, to pay her bills and to start saving for the future. Yes, a future. She also needed time to handle issues related to the order of protection against her husband and to file for divorce and to seek custody of little Mary. She also desperately needed to learn how to navigate the U.S. court system.

On top of all that, how was she going to concentrate on learning English? Learn to be a part of this new culture? Make her life permanent in the Chicago area? Become a U.S. citizen? It was overwhelming and her heart sped up. Maribel slowly shook her head.

Stop, she commanded herself. How far can this really go? She had no papers. No money. No driver's license. No car. No husband. And now, no luck. Her heart began to slow. Maribel looked at her feet and then glanced at the wide-eyed sorrowful look on Mary's face.

The social worker rang the doorbell of the center. They stood at the threshold of change in their lives.

Sister Kathleen and Sister Ann answered the door, smiled and led their guests inside. Maribel did not see old-fashioned nuns in long, black veils and long white habits with rosary beads dangling at their sides. Instead, these religious sisters had short hair and wore modern but conservative black skirts and white blouses with simple crosses hanging from their necks.

Maribel froze. She didn't want to become a student again. She was already ashamed that she abandoned her university education after getting married and leaving Mexico. Now, she was too busy trying to survive without her husband's income.

The social worker prodded Maribel along, and Maribel politely nodded a hello to each of the sisters and remained quiet.

Maribel heard the social worker rattle on in English to Sister Kathleen. She could become a student of one of the sisters at the literacy center. What about her daughter? Maribel could not afford a babysitter while she took English lessons. The social worker and sisters talked further. Mary could join her during the tutoring sessions as long as Maribel focused on the lessons and Mary did what she was told.

As the social worker began to arrange for sessions twice a week, Maribel wondered how much all of this would cost. She didn't have anything to spare.

"There's no cost to Maribel," Sister Kathleen said. Generous donations, grants and community support helped to sustain the center and students like Maribel.

Maribel remembered what her estranged husband once said, "How much you give is how much you will receive." During the time with her husband, Maribel didn't feel appreciated. His insults led her to believe that no one cared about her. But somehow, something was changing now.

Maribel looked around. Some of the women students who walked down the hallway had brown skin just like her. Their voices sounded like they also were from Mexico. Other languages were not familiar. It gave her some hope to be among people who seemed just like her.

She then resigned herself to taking the English lessons and to see where it would lead. Little did she realize her life would never be the same.

Chapter 8

JUANITA FINDS A NEW LANDING

For Juanita, the situation had become untenable. Months dragged by and she longed for her freedom to go outside without the fear of being kidnapped or raped by those young men who stalked her. She could not continue to live like a captive at home.

So, she decided to escape.

She finally told her family what was happening, and they quietly started making plans. They arranged for her to have a vacation with other family members in the Chicago area. It was a plan for her new life, away from her tormentors, that also offered better prospects for earning more money and living a better life.

How would she leave the house without being recognized, once their plan kicked into gear? Juanita had so few clothes of her own, that she would be instantly recognized by one of her stalkers. So, with the help of a sister, Juanita disguised herself by pulling on a wig and slipping into her sister's clothes. She also stuffed a few personal items into a bag and set it aside.

As darkness fell, the plan went into full gear.

Shaking, Juanita looked around and snuck out the back door. She paused briefly, wanting to deeply breathe in the smell of the cool night air. She wanted to capture every breath, every taste and every sound of the night air, because she thought it may be her last time in Mexico.

Then she jumped into a waiting car that included one of her sisters and drove directly to the airport in Mexico City. Once there, Juanita hugged that sister goodbye and boarded a plane for the United States. When she arrived at the Chicago airport, Juanita got a ride to Aurora, where she reunited with another sister. They hugged each other tight as they began to cry tears of joy. Juanita made it. She was safe.

She was at her new home and the start of a new life.

***

Once Juanita settled in, she got a job that paid about $70 a week to help pay the rent and her meals. She also saved some money, which she sent back to her parents in Mexico. But when Juanita later heard her mother was sick, she struggled with the decision on whether to rush to her side or stay safely in Aurora. If Juanita returned to Mexico, she could run into those men who had threatened to kidnap and to rape her. Chills again raced down her spine at the thought.

Still, Juanita felt her family was more important than herself and she returned to Mexico to see her mother. When she arrived in her hometown, Juanita learned that the four men, who tormented her, had moved on to other things, including to various cities in the United States. She was relieved. It was easier to relax now and to focus on helping her mother. She also returned to her old job at the shoe store.

After a while, Juanita's sister again sent her money for a ticket to return to Aurora. Juanita gladly accepted and felt it was time to move on with her life since her mother had improved. Juanita wanted to bring something new and better into her life and felt that opportunity was still waiting in Aurora.

***

After returning to Aurora, Juanita started a sewing job at a factory. She met more people and struck up several new friendships. Some new friends invited her to a house party where she met Jaime Rodriguez, who was no relation to her despite having the same last name.

He started talking to her, but Juanita quickly decided that she didn't like him. Jaime persisted. They eventually talked more and she gradually warmed up to him. Their name wasn't the only coincidence. They also lived in the same apartment building. Soon, their relationship blossomed, and they dated for about a year and a half.

Then, one evening as they sat in the stairwell of the

apartment building, Jaime proposed by pulling out an engagement ring from his pocket and presenting it to her. He eyed her cautiously, waiting for her response.

Surprised, Juanita looked at him and hesitated.

"I'll marry you only if you quit smoking," she said. "And we'll need to talk to my parents first."

Relieved, Jaime agreed to quit smoking, cold turkey, the next day.

When they talked with Juanita's parents, they were excited and blessed the upcoming marriage. They then started planning a traditional Catholic church wedding.

When the day arrived in 1981, at age 25, Juanita stood in her long white bridal gown next to Jaime, who wore a black tuxedo. During their wedding Mass, they professed their vows before a priest and later celebrated with their families at a reception.

They then settled into married life and attended church together every Sunday. Jaime also got a job with Standard Oil, first as a janitor and then, later, handling the stock room and ordering equipment.

***

After giving birth to their first daughter, Vanessa, Juanita decided it was time to start learning English. She wanted to be a part of American society and felt the best way to start was to attend English classes at the nearby Waubonsee Community

College. But sitting in a classroom for the first time in her life was hard. Still harder was her difficulty in grasping the language and her embarrassment in front of other students whenever she stumbled on pronunciations. When some students laughed at her mistakes, her heart ached with embarrassment. Despite this, she slowly picked up a few words.

She also found it difficult to write in English. Perhaps it was because she stayed home most of the time and rarely went outside or socialized with others who spoke English. She wasn't exposed to the language every day, like her husband, and felt she was losing ground. She eventually stopped going to the classes.

***

As the years passed, Juanita was taking care of two more children, Yesenia and Andy, and she relied more heavily on Jaime. When their children needed help with homework or needed a doctor, Jaime handled it because Juanita could not communicate their needs in English. Even when they needed food, Juanita asked Jaime to drive her to the grocery store.

Finally, Jaime insisted that Juanita at least learn how to drive. Juanita often avoided this topic, until Jaime put his foot down.

"You need to learn how to drive," Jaime said. "I cannot be here all the time. I cannot keep taking time off from work."

The thought of Jaime jeopardizing his job suddenly scared Juanita. If that happened, she would be poor again, scrounging for money to pay for food for her family and to pay bills and searching for ways to keep a roof over their heads. She relented. He knew her confidence was low, but her love for her husband was strong. It was enough to compel her to do what he asked.

A few days later, Juanita slid into the passenger seat of their Dodge Omni while Jaime sat behind the steering wheel to show her the accessories on the steering column and on the dash. He then drove her to an empty parking lot and they switched seats. It was strange at first, but Juanita got used to being behind the wheel, stepping on the gas and brake pedals and learning how to shift gears. She learned to drive the car forward and in reverse and how to park. She was careful to use the mirrors and watch for others nearby. They were all rudimentary steps, but important ones that she was finally grasping

Eventually, Juanita's practice paid off and she began feeling comfortable enough to have Jaime take her for a driver's license. When Juanita passed the driving test, a sense of relief washed over her. Freedom!

Juanita now could go anywhere she wanted at any time. She no longer had to wait for her husband to leave work to pick her up from anywhere. She did not have to jeopardize his job or their future together. She was now free to come and go, free to help her children when they needed something and free to even help herself.

But her freedom was still not entirely free. Juanita hesitated if she had to go to the grocery store. She froze if she tried to take her children to the doctor or even when she tried to read the street signs or ask for directions. Juanita was still unable to fully attain the freedom she wanted. She still needed Jaime to translate.

Juanita knew she needed help to learn English. She could not see herself continuing to rely on Jaime. And she had to stop asking nearby acquaintances, who acted as translators in a pinch. She knew it wasn't fair to keep imposing on anyone.

She easily left behind her independence in Mexico, only to find it much harder to regain it once she lived in the United States. It left her wondering: Did she make the right decision? The struggle of being a part of two worlds was becoming more difficult and she needed to make another decision to ensure she had a good future in only one world.

***

In 1993, Juanita and her family were attending Sunday Mass at her Catholic church, one of the few havens where she still felt safe from the echoes of the past, including that now far-away threat of those four men when she was living in Mexico.

Her ears perked up as a special speaker came forward to talk. It was Sister Kathleen, a longtime educator, who talked about forming the Dominican Literacy Center in Aurora that would teach English to immigrant women. The center would provide one-on-one instruction, so students could learn with customized lessons and better understand the language of their adopted country. Sister Kathleen also made a pitch seeking volunteer tutors, who were needed to help these students. Tutors would receive training and would need to devote time each week to prepare lessons for one student at a time.

Juanita, a slender, quiet woman, felt like she still lacked the basics of the English language. She also was no longer a child, but instead had children of her own, who needed a mother who could communicate with them and help them as they grew. But while they were speaking English more and more, Juanita felt that she lagged. It would be difficult to catch up with them the longer she let her situation continue. She initially thought all she had to do was to copy down everything she saw and just work hard to learn the words. That's how she did it when she was 11 years old and tried to learn things on her own, especially since her father didn't think it was necessary for children to go to school. As a result, Juanita still couldn't read or write. Yet when she saw how her sisters copied words from others and learned what they meant, she tried it as well. But she faltered. She felt now like she was reliving her past.

Juanita continued to listen to Sister Kathleen speak. But she was not like other sisters or nuns. Sister Kathleen wore regular clothes just like Juanita. She spoke directly to the people in a very straight-forward, businesslike yet friendly manner. She stood with dignity and grace.

Juanita felt like she was discovering something new. A

chance to learn English without a class full of students who might laugh at her mistakes. A chance to ask questions without being questioned herself. It seemed like a miracle. She perked up, smiled and turned to Jaime. He returned the smile, knowing exactly what was in his wife's mind.

That night, after their children were in bed, a quietness settled in the house and Juanita sighed. She was eager to bring up what was discussed at Mass earlier that day and sat down with Jaime to talk. Could this be a sign from God to try this new center and to learn English with a tutor?

"Sister Kathleen seems like she would be a good teacher," Jaime said. "You should look into taking those English lessons. It will help you."

"Yes, I know. I want to do this," Juanita replied.

Once she made the decision out loud, she felt a rush through her body. The mere act of agreeing to move ahead, to finally have an opportunity to learn English in a secure and safe setting, seemed to take a burden off her shoulders. After all, being part of a center that offered the instructions she needed could help her family and her own needs. And now with Jaime's blessings, she was free to inquire about it on Monday morning.

Then, just as quickly, she became nervous. Juanita knew, deep down, she lacked confidence. Could she fully learn a new language? Could it help her to fit into this new society? It was daunting. Juanita caught Jaime looking at her and realized she was questioning her own abilities again.

"You can do this," Jaime told her.

Juanita loved the way her husband supported her. He never wavered. She knew he had faith in her and that helped her to make the decision.

She thought of her children. When they needed help with homework, which was always written in English, Juanita could not help them. When her children needed to go to the doctor, who only spoke English, Jaime still was forced to take time off from work to be her translator. Taking time off work so frequently could jeopardize his job and their home.

She had to finally grab onto her American life and her new home and this new language. It was time.

Chapter 9

BLANCA IS EAGER FOR A NEW LIFE

In 1972, Blanca was 23 years old and felt it was time to pursue a dream — to live in the United States. Her brother, Roberto, was already living in Chicago and her father also traveled back and forth several times for work. Blanca longed to join them and she finally broke the news to her mother.

"Are you crazy?" Maria Gonzales said. "How are you going to leave me?"

"It's my dream to go to the United States, to stay by dad and Roberto," Blanca said.

A few months later, when her father returned home for a brief vacation, Blanca talked with him about moving to Chicago. Her mother did not want to join them, and Blanca didn't have enough money to try this venture by herself. Their discussion led to her Aunt Lilia and Uncle Chuy, who had a home in Aurora. Perhaps they could help ease her transition into a foreign country and help her to get on her feet financially. Blanca made the arrangements to live with them and took the leap.

After arriving in Aurora, Blanca loved the thrill of discovering this new country. She even started picking up a few words of English. But after three years, Blanca still struggled with the English language and decided to return to Mexico in 1975. But her experience in a new country and the hope of living the American dream was still attractive her. She could not let go of that dream just yet.

In 1980, Blanca returned to the United States and it was just as exciting as the first time. She felt safe and people were nice to her. This time, the Chicago area became her second home as she parlayed her sewing expertise into a job at a coat factory, where her aunt also worked. Blanca became a part of an assembly line that made raincoats and heavy winter coats.

While others on the line attached various parts of the coat, she attached the sleeves. Another worker pushed a cart up and down the aisles, picked up the boxes of finished coats and then automatically handed out other boxes with unfinished parts. The coat factory was busy, and she enjoyed working with a diverse group of people, including African Americans, Puerto Ricans, Greeks and others. It was an international line and they all worked together to complete their tasks each day. It made the days easier while Blanca saved her wages for the future.

That same year, Blanca attended a community dance, where she met Eusebio, who was originally from Durango, Mexico. Their eyes met and it was love at first sight when Eusebio asked her to dance. By the end of the evening, she gave her phone number to Eusebio and he later called her.

They often got together on the weekends at Phillips Park in Aurora or met with friends over the next year and a half.

As their relationship progressed, Eusebio wanted to speak to Blanca's father before he moved back to Mexico for his retirement. Eusebio asked Blanca's father for her hand in marriage and her father gave his permission. Eusebio then formally proposed to Blanca and gave her a gold ring with a diamond, which she happily slipped onto her finger.

They married on a rainy day in October 1981. As she entered Sacred Heart Catholic Church in Aurora, Blanca wore a traditional long white bridal gown designed with lace and pearls and a crown of flowers with a long flowing veil. After the wedding Mass, they reveled in a large reception with their friends and family. They decided not to have a honeymoon, and instead, Eusebio returned to work where he fixed golf carts and other equipment at a nearby company.

During those early years, they continued to live in Aurora and she later registered for classes at Waubonsee Community College to learn how to speak and to write English. Since she did not have a car, she walked five blocks to the school.

In the meantime, Blanca also received her permanent U.S. residency and wanted to get on the path to U.S. citizenship. It was something she eagerly sought because it would fulfill another part of her dream.

Blanca already fulfilled another dream by marrying Eusebio and then starting a family. Blanca went through back-breaking labor to deliver their first-born daughter, Diana, in 1982. Caring for a baby while holding down a job created a new balancing act for Blanca. She frequently asked friends and relatives for rides to the babysitter. It then became more difficult when they couldn't provide a ride due to myriad reasons. Like so many times in her life, Blanca knew when she needed to make a change. That's when she began to focus on how to drive a car.

Driving a car would help Blanca to get her daughter to the babysitter and then she could go straight to work, instead of being dependent on other people, their schedules or the unreliability of their cars. Blanca got a lesson from Eusebio on how to turn on the engine and drive up and down about three blocks. She later practiced with their older-model car.

In 1983, she felt ready to get her license and headed to the driver's license facility. She was nervous during the driving test, but she passed. And she quickly chalked up yet another milestone in her life in the United States. Now, she was able to drive herself to and from the babysitter's home and to her job. ... All the while, she kept a Bible on the front passenger seat.

***

By 1985, Blanca decided it was time to complete her goal of becoming a U.S. citizen and to become a more integral part of the United States. She enrolled at Waubonsee Community College, this time for classes that would help her to prepare for the U.S. citizenship test.

When the day came to take the test, she left her late-shift job, went home and attempted to sleep. But she was too excited and could only catch a few hours of rest. She then traveled to downtown Chicago to take the test and felt nervous about what this new gateway to the future would hold.

"To stand in front of people in Immigration was not easy," Blanca later told Eusebio. "I had to open my eyes and ears to catch the questions."

She passed the test and later received a letter in the mail that said she passed her test to become a U.S. citizen. Now, the last step was at hand: taking the oath of citizenship.

Eusebio drove Blanca to the federal courthouse in downtown Chicago, so she could join dozens of others who also were ready to take that final leap. Together, they all recited the oath of U.S. citizenship:

I hereby declare, on oath, that I absolutely and entirely renounce and abjure all allegiance and fidelity to any foreign prince, potentate, state or sovereignty, of whom or which I have heretofore been a subject or citizen; that I will support and defend the Constitution and laws of the United States of America against all enemies, foreign and domestic; that I will bear true faith and allegiance to the same; that I will bear arms on behalf of the United States when required by the law; that I will perform noncombatant service in the Armed Forces of the United States when required by the law; that I will perform work of national importance under civilian direction when required by the law; and that I take this obligation freely, without any mental reservation or purpose of evasion; so help me God.

Suddenly, Blanca was excited. She realized another goal was completed.

She and Eusebio returned to their home in the Fox Valley. It was just like any other day. But then again, it wasn't. She now could experience a new level of freedom that she never had before, including a chance to vote in the U.S. elections. It was the first day she was a citizen of the United States. She belonged.

***

By 1987, Blanca gave birth to twins, a daughter named Rocio and a son named Ricardo. Managing the newborns was a challenge while also chasing after little Diana. Although Eusebio helped with the babies and the household, Blanca knew that she had to change to a later shift at work.

The following year, Blanca found a job as a second-shift housekeeper at a medical clinic in Aurora. She vacuumed carpets, washed floors, dusted shelves and desks, emptied wastebaskets, among other cleaning duties.

After about a year, she was promoted to an assistant supervisor. She always liked the idea of being a leader and this gave her a taste of what it was like to be a boss. She enjoyed the new title and responsibilities. Mostly, she welcomed the chance to learn more and to earn additional income. That extra money helped her family and Blanca loved the work. She was a strong believer that if you liked what you do, you will do it well.

Her next goal was to aim for the top supervisor's position.

Chapter 10

TERESA MAKES THE MOVE

Teresa's pregnancy was unexpected but welcomed news. To help prepare for their new family, Miguel decided he needed to make more money and crossed the U.S. border to get a job picking cotton in Texas. But he was undocumented and U.S. immigration deported him to Mexico.

Still, Miguel tried to enter the United States again, this time arriving in the Chicago area. He got a job planting and tending flowers at a nursery in Aurora. He then applied for a green card and continued to live in the area. Teresa stayed behind in Mexico City with their daughter, Elizabeth.

Over the next few years, Miguel continued to work in the United States and returned home to visit his family. They soon had sons Jorge and Miguel. The children loved their father, so it was tough to see him return to the United States to work. As Teresa and the children remained in Mexico City, she felt more and more isolated without Miguel.

Finally, Teresa decided to take the plunge and left Mexico to join Miguel in Aurora. While the reunion was good, she soon found herself growing sadder each day because it was difficult to communicate with others. Her confidence plummeted.

Trying to become acclimated to a new country with a different language was harder than she expected. Teresa felt under more stress because she didn't understand English — especially if she needed to take her children to the doctor or when they needed help with their homework. She didn't know what to say. Dealing with nurses, doctors, teachers and others who only knew English made her feel even more alone.

Chapter 11

MARIA OVERCOMES OBSTACLES

After Maria gave birth to her daughter, Paola, she stopped working and took care of her full time in Mexico City. During that time, Valentin worked as a subcontractor who fixed underground cables for a telecommunications company. But he wasn't earning enough money to support his growing family.

Maria didn't have the money to buy clothes for herself and her daughter or to buy good, quality food. That's when she talked to Valentin about going to the United States to earn more money for their family and to save some extra cash to help support his mother. She also suggested that he could establish a home there. Then, after a year or so, she and Paola could move there. Or he could save the money and come back and do other work, like drive a taxi. She convinced him that her plan to work in the United States was the best option.

***

When Valentin arrived in the Chicago area, he lived with a relative of Maria's father and worked as a landscaper. Since landscaping was seasonal work, Valentin found a factory job during the winter. But he soon discovered that trying to get to work without a car during the brutal winters was difficult.

In the winter of 1988, Maria got visas for herself and her daughter, who was 3 years old, and they traveled to Chicago. They arrived in the United States and moved in with an aunt in Aurora for a few months. Valentin joined them and they saved money until they could afford their own apartment.

While living in Aurora, Maria walked everywhere because she did not know how to drive. She even walked to the grocery store and lugged the heavy bags of food back home. One store was just across the street from their apartment and another store was a few blocks away. Both stores were owned by the same man. Maria felt her family needed extra income, so she approached the grocery store owner for a job.

After she was hired, Maria found a babysitter for her daughter so she could work the noon-to-9 p.m. shift. After cleaning and locking up the grocery store for the night, she walked to pick up her daughter from the babysitter and headed home. The darkness and the area still seemed foreign to her and it prompted Maria to walk swiftly.

One night, a car slowly drove past them and the driver side

window was lowered. The driver asked them if they wanted a ride. Maria's heart nearly stopped. Her daughter, sensing Maria's fear in the darkness, started to scream. The driver sped off as she ran the rest of the way home. She then slammed and locked the door behind her. Breathless, she stood silently, checking to see if anyone followed her to the door. Luckily, no one was there and she breathed a sigh of relief.

That's when she decided to talk to Valentin.

"We need to buy a car," Maria said.

"But how will we pay for it?" Valentin asked.

"I will find a way," Maria said.

The next day, Maria asked the owner of the grocery store for a $2,000 loan. The owner agreed and offered the loan interest free. But he told her that he would take the money out of her paycheck each week until the loan was paid.

Maria quickly brought the $2,000 home and placed it on the kitchen table. Now that they had the cash in hand, she and Valentin decided to call someone they had heard was selling a car. They quickly made arrangements to see the car and Valentin drove it home that night.

Maria also used that same car to learn how to drive. She learned to love that car because it brought her a new freedom that she never felt before and it fueled her desire to get a driver's license. But there was clearly more to learn than she realized.

So, Valentin took Maria to a nearby empty parking lot to teach her how to drive. She barely got the car in gear and drove a few yards when Valentin stopped her.

"Oh no, you are hitting too many cars already," Valentin said.

"But the lot is empty," Maria said.

"You have to think there are cars here, so you won't hit the cars in the street," he said.

The next day at work, Valentin happened to mention to a woman co-worker how he brought his wife out for a driving lesson.

"You don't have enough patience with her," the co-worker said. "I will teach her."

So, Valentin's co-worker took Maria out early the next weekend around the Fox Valley Mall. After a few hours, Maria was able to drive. A few weeks later, Maria went for her driver's license, but failed because she didn't stop the car properly. Maria knew she needed to practice and devoted herself to improving her skills.

"You should stop, look around and then go," Valentin's co-worker told her.

She also knew that she needed to try for the license again soon or she would lose her confidence. Maria continued to practice and then returned to the driver's facility to take the driver's test again.

This time, Maria passed. She was thrilled, not just because she was getting her first U.S. driver's license, but because it meant an extra measure of safety for her at night when she went after work to pick up their daughter. It also would make life much easier, since she now had transportation to the grocery store, to the laundromat and other errands. Maria was relieved and thrilled at the same time. Now, she could do more for her family in an efficient way.

A month later, the car's transmission blew out and Maria and Valentin worried about finding the money for the repair. Instead, they went without a car until they could save enough to buy another one.

***

On Thanksgiving Day, Maria was making tamales and waiting for Valentin to come home from work by 10 p.m. But he did not arrive.

By 11 p.m., Maria was worried. She had no phone to call Valentin and she constantly went to the front door to check. Then someone knocked on the front door and her adrenaline surged. Maria saw her cousin, Salvador, through the window.

"We have bad news," Salvador told Maria. "Your husband is in the hospital."

Valentin was driving the landscaping company's truck when the brakes apparently failed and it was struck by another vehicle. The other driver checked Valentin's pockets to get an emergency contact and found Salvador's number.

After Salvador left, Maria crumbled into tears. She became terrified as questions flooded her mind. What should she do? How could she get to her husband? She had to stop and think clearly and quickly.

The landlord of the house, where Maria rented, became concerned when he heard voices so late at night. He then found Maria in tears. He reassured Maria that they would get her to the hospital some way so she could be with her husband. He then checked with his son, hoping he could drive Maria. But, the young man could not. Instead, the landlord used his own phone and found another relative to drive her.

When Maria reached the hospital room, fear sent a chill through her. She saw Valentin lying motionless in the bed with several tubes connected to him and machines surrounding him. She froze. By now, it was 1 a.m. and the lack of sleep and the fear of the unknown gripped her. She sat in a chair near his bed and watched him for hours.

Finally, near dawn, Valentin opened his eyes, turned his head slightly and saw his wife.

"Don't cry," Valentin said to Maria.

"I'm OK," Maria said. "I love you!"

As Valentin gradually improved, the hospital released him,

and Maria arranged to have someone drive them home. He needed to use crutches and was prescribed physical therapy for several months.

As the medical bills poured in, Maria temporarily became the sole breadwinner and worked 10 hours a day, seven days a week at the grocery store. It was hard to pay the rent, food and other bills with her paycheck. But they scraped by and she made sure everything was paid.

***

While working at the grocery store, Maria noticed that most of the customers spoke Spanish. So, she felt no rush to learn English. However, when she got a new job cutting fabric samples at a factory in west suburban Montgomery, she had difficulty communicating with her co-workers.

There was an American woman who was cutting fabric at a long table and only talked to Maria in English. Since Maria didn't know English, she decided to take a notebook and write down some of her words that she later showed to Valentin. He then translated those words for her.

Without knowing English, Maria felt isolated. She wasn't picking up English as easily as her husband was from his co-workers. And she was at a disadvantage when taking her children to the doctor and trying to communicate with the staff, which led her to asking Valentin to accompany them. She felt bad that he had to take time off from work just to translate for her, again and again. That made her feel useless and insignificant. It also was embarrassing when she always needed Valentin to translate in other matters as well, as if she were stupid and could not do anything for herself.

But Maria knew she wasn't stupid.

***

Maria and Valentin worked together well when it came to running the household and saving money. By 1992, they had saved enough for a down payment and qualified for a 30-year mortgage to buy their first one-bedroom home in Aurora. It was small, but it was mighty to them because it meant leaving behind rent. It also offered a sense of permanence in a new society — a part of the American dream — and a symbol of a solid family. While it was daunting, it was exciting, and they just knew their small home would work well for them.

Now, their children could run around the house to their heart's content without disrupting anyone. When they put the key in the door, they knew it was all theirs, regardless of its size. The kids slept in the one bedroom, while Maria and Valentin slept in the living room. It was enough for right now.

A retired couple, who lived next door, stopped by to introduce themselves. Maria was still cautious around Americans, mostly because they would realize that she could not speak English. But they were nice people, and they offered a warm welcome to them. Maria was finally feeling like this could be home.

Chapter 12

THE CENTER GETS ITS FIRST STUDENT

Excited about her order's approval of the literacy center, Sister Kathleen's attention returned to the check she received from her community. She then began to make a quick list in her mind of what she needed to do. She started making phone calls to seek information and advice on where this new ministry was needed the most. She then talked with priests, other church ministers and social service groups familiar with the east side of Aurora, where the Hispanic immigrant population appeared to be exploding.

Without exception, she heard that the most underserved population in Aurora was immigrant women. They were usually the last in their families to learn English. Their children learned English at school and acclimated quickly. Many of their husbands learned English at Waubonsee Community College or they picked up the language from co-workers on their jobs.

But most of the women who worked outside of their homes had housekeeping or factory jobs with other immigrant women. Their opportunities to learn English, and to use it frequently, appeared to be minimal.

These women also, achingly, realized they could not help their children with their homework. They did not understand what their children said in English. They could not shop in the local grocery store or go to the doctor alone, since their husbands or children were their interpreters, and they were gone most of the day. Those everyday errands, or otherwise simple situations, were causing these women to feel disconnected within their own homes and communities. That led to an erosion of self-worth and self-esteem that acerbated their abilities to fit into the community.

One immigrant woman told Sister Kathleen that every day she felt that she was being "erased." The woman then raised her arm and fanned it across an imaginary blackboard as if erasing her language and her life. Sister Kathleen did not want to see anyone erased, especially when they had so much to contribute to their families, to the community and to God.

Aurora had an immigrant population since the 1920s and 1930s and the local population was growing even faster now. Anything that could be done to streamline their entry into society would help them and the community. Sister Kathleen was convinced that the east side of Aurora was where she should establish the Dominican Literacy Center.

Sister Kathleen then met Bertha Manzo, a secretary for the Aurora Deanery, one of the groupings that included parishes in the archdiocese. She also met Eva Cruz, a coordinator of ministry and evangelization. Their offices were in the former convent of St. Nicholas Parish in Aurora, and they offered Sister Kathleen a portion of the basement for her use. Bertha also suggested that she could help Sister Kathleen connect with women who wanted to learn English.

Once the location was secured, Sister Kathleen's plan was to use the 1993–1994 school year to set up the curriculum, to train volunteer tutors and, most of all, to research and to apply for grants to fund the new Dominican Literacy Center. From July to September, Sister Kathleen took the commuter train to the Donors Forum of Chicago, based in downtown Chicago, in order to look through collections of books that listed funders by mission, geography and preferred projects. She then set up a portable IBM Selectric typewriter, snuggled on a towel to keep it steady, while she worked in the dining room of St. Peter's convent to complete the grant forms. She sent completed forms and other supporting materials to the Raskob Foundation, the Conrad N. Hilton Fund for Sisters and the Dominican Fathers Midwest Province.

Soon, contributions began arriving and she eventually garnered about $20,000. It was enough to start the first year.

She then decided it was time to get the word out to the community by placing advertisements in local church bulletins and talking about the new center during Sunday Masses at the local churches.

***

Sister Kathleen was at St. Nicholas when Bertha told her that some women were eager to learn English. Sister Kathleen smiled. It felt good to know that potential students were ready to sign up. They either heard Sister Kathleen speak at some Sunday Masses or saw a notice in their church bulletins. Sister Kathleen was just happy that word was beginning to spread.

She told Bertha that she would start tutoring in September of next year.

"But," Bertha said, "One of them is here now and she wants to start!"

Sister Kathleen didn't expect the center to take off so soon. So, she met with the women to see if she could do a quick inventory of their skills and how she could accommodate them.

The first was Juanita Rodriguez, who wanted to start that day. But Sister Kathleen said she needed to organize her lessons and order books and materials. She encouraged Juanita to return the following week.

Juanita eagerly returned that next week and began her first tutoring session in the St. Nicholas basement while sitting on an old folding chair at a rickety card table. Juanita, who was working as a night-shift housekeeper at a medical clinic, made sure she had the time during the day to do the English lessons.

For Juanita, it was a chance to change her life and forget those days of being excluded whenever someone spoke English or when her children wanted her help. She no longer wanted to feel helpless. Most of all, it would ensure that she could become a more integral part of American society. Although Juanita was nervous and unsure of herself, she was eager to know what was ahead of her. She was ready.

During the tutoring lesson, Sister Kathleen sat across from Juanita as they started with the English words for colors, numbers and a few basic conversational words. She then asked Juanita to put them into sentences and practice saying those sentences. She was learning how each of those words had their own place in the language.

Juanita returned twice a week. While many of the one-and-a-half-hour sessions were in the basement, some were held upstairs in an office. But it didn't matter where they were. Juanita was learning. Sister Kathleen was very clear on how she presented the material each week and Juanita felt she was starting to make progress. For the first time, Juanita felt encouraged and she was excited when she grasped the words that before seemed so elusive. She was also becoming so diligent that she nearly wore out her Target Spelling 360 Book.

As the weeks continued, Juanita made cookies or a cake and brought them to her lessons to share with the handful of other women students who recently signed up. It soon became a tradition that continued even as more new students and volunteer tutors joined the center.

Juanita gradually became more comfortable around Sister Kathleen and trusted that she would point her in the right direction. It felt very natural when she started talking to Sister Kathleen about her family. Juanita felt that no matter what she talked about with Sister Kathleen, it stayed between them. The two women were from different cultures, different customs and different environments. Yet, they were bonding, something Juanita never experienced before. Juanita no longer felt intimidated or anxious or nervous. Something was changing inside of her ... for the better.

"I know I can talk with you and not be afraid," Juanita told Sister Kathleen after they closed their workbooks. "Now, no one laughs at me. You made me very strong and I trust you very much. I also learned a lot on how to be a good wife and a good person and, especially, to not be afraid. I also learned to open up a lot. I learned I can say what I want, talk in English and no one will laugh at me."

"That's because you can do this," Sister Kathleen said. "You just had to discover it for yourself."

Juanita already had a composition notebook packed with such encouraging notes from Sister Kathleen, including compliments about her work. "Wonderful work, Juanita. I'm very proud of you!" said one note from November 1993. Then there was another: "This is wonderful! What a great writer you are becoming!" Those notes deeply moved Juanita. She never experienced such encouragement from someone, other than her husband.

Another time, Juanita was at her wit's end with one of her children and started to cry during a session. Juanita reassured Sister Kathleen that it wasn't anything she said. It was the stress of her children growing up and growing away from her. Life was changing again. Sister Kathleen then soothed Juanita with comforting words … in English.

For the first time, Juanita actually felt the words, instead of just speaking them. They were powerful. They hit home, deep into her heart.

If words can make you feel such emotions, then Juanita needed to know more. She had to keep learning all she could so she, too, could help others.

***

Besides Juanita, another early student at the center was

Esperanza Leos, who already learned some English just by listening to others. Her parents were farm pickers, who moved from state to state to get work. Esperanza and her husband worked on a horse farm in nearby Plainfield, Illinois. They had two children and later bought a house in Aurora.

When her husband died, Esperanza became a housekeeper at Sacred Heart Parish. She cleaned the rectory and did the grocery shopping for the parish priest, Father Tim Piasecki. But she couldn't read Spanish or English.

She told Sister Kathleen that her goals were to learn to read the shopping list that Father Tim made for her, to read the hymns in the songbook at Mass and to read the Bible.

Esperanza became like a grandmother to many young women who later arrived on the doorstep of the Dominican Literacy Center. She dispensed advice and encouragement to many of them. Esperanza also continued to study with the sisters for about 10 years, ignoring their policy that the program was just for three years.

Finally, Esperanza could read English well. She loved reading her mail, funny stories, and most of all, the Bible.

PART 3
CHOOSING TO FLY

Chapter 13

MARIBEL LEARNS LESSONS ABOUT LIFE

When Maribel reported to her first tutoring session, Sister Ann showed her the dining room where a large photocopier was nestled between the front window and a large wooden dining room table. The kitchen had older white appliances while a box loaded with homemade cookies, free to all, was on a nearby counter. Down the hall was a living room that was turned into a meeting room with an old sofa and plenty of metal folding chairs, a staple since Sister Kathleen started the center.

Maribel nodded to Sister Ann as they walked by each doorway. The rooms made her feel comfortable, and strangely, at peace, possibly because she imagined the sisters praying there. Or because they welcomed students before her and she no longer felt like she was the only one who had walked through that front door. The lessons, the sincerity to learn, and the structure of the setting emitted an intimacy that reached deep into Maribel's soul.

Sister Ann led Maribel into a small room, once used as a bedroom by a religious sister. It now contained a small desk and a round wooden table, a closet and a white pedestal sink. While the two women sat across from each other at the table, Sister Ann invited Maribel's daughter, Mary, to sit on the floor with some coloring books and crayons.

"Here, Mary, I want you to draw some beautiful pictures for your mama," Sister Ann said. The little girl smiled, grabbed the crayons, selected her colors and began to draw.

Maribel turned to her tutor as Sister Ann gave Maribel a workbook. They began looking at pictures and repeating words in English.

As the classes continued over the weeks, Maribel fumbled over words, and then she shyly looked up at Sister Ann.

"Maribel, you know how to do it, just try," Sister Ann said.

Maribel tried again, aiming to get the right words in the right order. She diligently followed the pictures during class.

Elsewhere, she listened to strangers talk and even used some English when going through the checkout lane at the grocery store. She built her sentences one word at a time, one breath at a time. Slowly, Maribel was gaining confidence.

Some days, Maribel brought homework to do before she went to her night-shift job. She often did the work in front of Mary. When she struggled, Maribel would shyly look at her daughter, who quickly picked up English during her kindergarten classes. It seemed effortless for her little girl.

Maribel thought she could lean on Mary for guidance on some of the words. But the youngster shook her head.

"It's your homework, mommy, not mine," Mary said. Maribel's eyebrows shot up.

Another time, Mary insisted that they just speak English at home.

"I'm sorry, but I don't understand Spanish," Mary teased her mother.

Maribel continued to lean heavily on an English-Spanish dictionary to translate words. Some days were fraught with stress, as Maribel flipped pages like a fan, back and forth, trying to find the right word. Yet it was never quick enough. Yet, she would find the word and it would stay with her.

Even when Maribel went to work, she carried a small notebook. She pretended to clean the mirrors on the bathroom walls by using a circular motion with her hand while holding a cleaning rag. The action seemed to make her invisible to customers entering the bathroom. It allowed her to listen intently to the conversations of the women who used the toilet stalls or touched up their hair and makeup in front of the mirror. When they left, Maribel wrote down their words phonetically. She then stashed the notebook in her pocket, away from the eyes of her micro-managing boss.

"This means this," Maribel thought. She learned word by word.

Maribel continued to go twice a week for English lessons with Sister Ann, who often used a workbook and some magazines. She would have Maribel look at the photos and describe what she liked, tell her why or even ask how she would change the picture.

"Don't worry, try it," Sister Ann urged. "Don't be afraid."

Maribel especially liked when Sister Ann reassured her by saying: "No one will laugh at you."

The words were encouraging and meant the world to Maribel. No one would laugh. Or ridicule her.

Just then, echoes of her husband haunted her. How dare she try to improve herself.

"You are a failure," he used to say to Maribel. "You are less than nothing." His voice taunted her, even dared her to change, confident she would not do it.

Maribel then recalled a time when her husband went into another fit of rage, pulled apart the frame of a window, ripped out an aluminum rod, and used it to repeatedly hit her mouth and nose. Then, with an immense force, he picked her up and threw her into an open closet. When her body slammed inside, her blood splattered the closet's interior walls.

Their little girl, who was outside the bedroom door, cried

for help. Her husband's friends also stood outside. But no one came to rescue her. She did get a glimpse of their horrified looks when they saw her bloodied face in that split second when the vibrations of her crash landing accidentally opened the bedroom door. Maribel swallowed her screams with each impact. Maribel felt like a coward because she did not defend herself. She felt helpless as her daughter watched her mother being beaten on that horrible day.

At other times, her husband used to take the clothes she had just washed and ironed and laughingly tossed them on the floor, stomped all over them and insisted that she clean and iron them again. And there were countless times when she was afraid to smile or speak, for fear of setting him off, all over again, to either humiliate her or to beat her.

It was during a particularly bloody beating that Maribel frantically ran to a neighbor's house to call 911. At that time, she did not know English. So, when the dispatcher answered her call by speaking English, Maribel did not know what to say. Despite hanging up on the call, the police arrived in the neighborhood, much to Maribel's surprise. That's when Maribel saw her chance. She ran out of the house so fast that her husband was stunned. She spoke in Spanish to the Hispanic police officer about what happened, which then led to her husband's arrest, and later, to an order of protection.

But that was in the past. Maribel now returned to the present and focused more intently on her tutoring session with Sister Ann. Maribel squeezed her eyes shut and took a slow breath. She put aside those nightmares.

She had a new direction now. A new meaning for life. And the English words began to flow.

***

Maribel sat in the law offices of Patrick Kinnally, who came highly recommended and elicited respect based on his work and education. He earned a bachelor's degree cum laude from Loyola University and a law degree from John Marshall Law School. Besides winning cases with verdicts in the millions of dollars, he was a former examiner, attorney and instructor for the U.S. Immigration and Naturalization Service.

She never hired a lawyer before. Hiring a lawyer meant she was serious about severing all ties with her abusive husband. She also was living in a shelter, far from her husband's brutal reach and with little chance of him touching her again. Still, she worried how her life would change and how it would affect Mary.

Maribel was not fluent enough in English to easily answer questions and felt at a disadvantage when dealing with the translator sitting nearby. She did not know the translator or the lawyer and wondered if what she was saying was really being translated correctly. Was it being expressed with all the pain that she felt inside? Did they know her words choked in her throat? She looked down often, not wanting to make contact with either man and hoping this whole episode in her life would suddenly disappear.

Then, she straightened her back. She was there for two reasons: to divorce her husband and to ensure that he pay child support for their daughter. Whatever it took to protect her daughter, she would do it. She was finished with her husband this time. She was done with the endless fear of whether she would live or die; through with her daughter watching her mother get beaten again; finished with needing to heal from black eyes, broken bones and humiliation.

Now, she wanted to be completely free of her husband. Those horrors needed to end. Patrick interrupted Maribel's thoughts and brought her back to the present.

"I want to know whether you plan to go through with this," said Patrick. "There will be a lot of court dates involving the divorce, the order of protection, Mary's custody and support. Are you up to doing all of that?"

Patrick eyed Maribel, wondering if she was serious. Some abused women never went through with a divorce because they were afraid of their husbands, afraid of splitting apart their families, afraid of destitution and an unknown future.

Maribel nodded to the translator.

"I will not quit," Maribel said softly, looked at both men and then looked down.

It was that flash in Maribel's eyes that caught Patrick off guard. A spark of hate? Determination? A new-found sense of confidence? Kinnally hesitated. He saw too many women like this who were mentally and physically abused and who lost their self-esteem and self-worth. Yet, it was the way Maribel nodded that gave Patrick the encouragement to move forward with the case. Maribel appeared determined to break free, despite any cost.

"OK, Maribel. I will file the necessary papers and the court dates will be set. We will keep in touch," Patrick said.

Maribel turned to the translator, listened and nodded again.

"I do not want alimony," Maribel then told the translator. "I do not want anything else from my husband. I want nothing more to do with him."

"Are you sure, Maribel?" Patrick asked, turning away from the translator to address Maribel directly. "How will you support yourself?" The translator followed up and Maribel paused.

"I will find a way," Maribel said to the translator.

She slowly got up and moved toward the door, hesitated and then walked out. She knew she was walking away from her husband and away from a life of abuse.

***

After that day in the lawyer's office, each day brought more fears. Without enough money, Maribel barely put food on the table with her minimum-wage job of scrubbing toilets at Marshall Field's. She often resorted to taking day-old bagels from the lined trash can behind the retailer's bakery, looking around to make sure no one saw her and then wolfing them down. She did not want to tell her daughter what she did. Maribel tried to hide the sad parts because she did not want Mary to feel hopeless. Maribel pretended nothing was wrong, even after she learned of the court dates that were scheduled, along with some postponements. As the long months dragged on, everything blurred together.

During one major proceeding, the Kane County Circuit Court judge called up Maribel and her husband at the same time. While they stood together before the judge, they listened to the translator explain the rest of the court dates to dissolve the marriage. Once the judge was finished, Maribel and her husband turned to go back to their seats.

At that moment, Maribel's husband leaned over to her and whispered, "I will kill you."

Maribel visibly shuddered.

The judge saw what appeared to be a menacing threat by Maribel's husband and stopped them both. He first called up Maribel separately. The judge turned to the translator and asked what was just said between the couple and Maribel relayed her husband's threat. The judge immediately called a police officer to the bench and ordered Maribel's husband be taken into custody.

Maribel knew another arrest would further fuel her husband's hatred. She feared more than ever that her life was at risk. She went home in tears. When would these court dates be over? When would their relationship finally end so she could have control over her own life? Each time she returned to court, there was something else to worry about, even if her husband did not appear at the appointed time.

Maribel even questioned if she was able to finish the case. Was it time to stop the divorce? She went to her counselor, Christina, for advice and the counselor immediately became agitated.

"If you quit now, there won't be a next time," Christina said. "If you go back to him, and he beats you again, no one will get involved. No one will help you. Think about your daughter. Think about what will happen to her if he kills you."

Maribel felt lost and despondent and her head dropped down. She was in a foreign land with a foreign language. She wasn't close to anyone. She was like a nomad in Aurora, looking to transition to a stable life, especially for Mary. Both mother and daughter were sharing a bed, living by someone else's strict schedule, including meals at a set time and a curfew at night.

Still, the situation was better than having Mary watch her mother's blood splatter the walls or long recoveries from broken bones and black eyes.

"It will be better to be divorced than to live the way you had in the past," Christina said firmly.

A co-worker later opened her home to Maribel and Mary, so they could live a bit more freely, instead of abiding by the shelter's rules. But that arrangement soon soured when the woman's daughters fought with Mary and hid food from them.

Maribel knew it was time to find another place — a haven away from the fighting. Maribel found another place to live in Aurora. It was sparse, but she furnished it with items that acquaintances provided or she found in thrift stores.

**

During the winter, traveling on the bus was slow. Snow and ice made the trek difficult when Maribel left work, picked up her daughter from the babysitter and headed to the Dominican Literacy Center.

Then one day, Maribel quietly stopped going.

After two weeks, Maribel received a call from Sister Kathleen, who was checking to see if they were OK and why they had stopped coming for English lessons. Maribel explained how difficult it was to take the bus in the winter, pick up her daughter and then walk several blocks to the center.

"Well, we could help you. If you write a letter to give us permission, we can pick up your daughter from school or the babysitter and bring her here," Sister Kathleen said. Maribel agreed.

Mary went to the babysitter's home after her kindergarten sessions. Then, Sister Ann drove to the babysitter's home to pick up Mary twice a week before Maribel's English lesson. Maribel then was able to meet her connecting buses and arrive earlier for her tutoring session. Maribel, Mary and others were welcomed at the center with hot cocoa or soup to warm them before their lessons started.

Again, Sister Ann kept little Mary busy with activities. One time, Sister Ann even let Mary brush her hair into pig tails. They all laughed at the lopsided hair design.

When Sister Ann drove them home, she sometimes stopped at McDonald's, just so Mary could get a Happy Meal and collect the small toy inside. They were among the few toys the little girl played with that gave her joy and comfort and helped to fuel her imagination. Maribel was aware of that, so much so, that when they got home, they saved the small toy in a box along with others they collected.

Maribel went to the kitchen and opened the refrigerator. Only a gallon of water and a gallon of milk were inside. Two cookies were left on the counter. The cabinets were empty. As hungry as Maribel was, she was hoping the soup at the literacy center would sustain them. So, she offered just one cookie to Mary.

"But mommy, what will you eat," Mary said.

"I'm OK. You will eat this one now and have the other tomorrow for lunch at school," Maribel said.

Mary looked at the cookies and refused. She insisted that her mommy have one. Instead, they both began to cry. Maribel looked at an old Christmas tree propped up in a bucket in the living room. Her job only provided minimum wage, and that money was already earmarked for rent and other bills. She feared that without enough money to buy food, or even Christmas presents, it could be a longer winter than she anticipated.

A few days later, Sister Ann and Sister Kathleen parked outside of Maribel's apartment and rang her doorbell. Maribel answered the door with a look of surprise. The unexpected visit sent Maribel and Mary into a whirlwind of activity. They threw on some sweaters and ran out into the cold winter air. They were quickly enlisted to help carry some large plastic bags from the car's trunk into the house. Once inside, the two sisters asked the mother and daughter to open the bags.

Confused, Maribel looked at the sisters and then at the black bags. Mary started digging inside and pulled out donated packages of towels, cups, plates, dish detergent, soap and even

cereal, milk and meat. Also, there were clothes for both of them
— real Christmas presents! Maribel was stunned.

"We didn't have anything to offer you before, but now we
have enough that my mother can cook for you," Mary told the
sisters.

"That's OK. Mary, we could just use some glasses of water,"
said Sister Ann.

Mary ran to get the glasses of water, while the two sisters
started putting away the groceries.

"This is too much food," said Mary.

"Well, we know you will finish all of it," said Sister Ann,
as the two sisters filled the barren cabinets with food and
household necessities.

Maribel felt the two sisters were angels coming at just the
right time. Maribel turned to go to another room, where she
cried silently. It was a practice she learned all too well after her
husband beat her. But Mary, looking to tell her mother about yet
another gift, entered the living room and saw her mother crying.
Young Mary knew her mother was not upset this time. These
were different kinds of tears and they gave Mary a new sense of
peace. Mary was always in fear of her father, but now that fear
was slowly dissipating, especially as the sisters arrived to help fill
their lives.

The sisters also saw the sad Christmas tree, leaning in a
bucket in the living room, and asked about decorations.

"We have no ornaments," said Maribel.

Sister Ann paused, then said, "Yes, you do. What about those toys from the Happy Meals?"

Mary ran to the box and unloaded the small, colorful plastic toys onto the floor. They found some string and twist ties and latched the toys to the balding branches. Maribel watched her angels decorate the tree and realized they had taught her more than English.

They taught her about love without fear.

***

By February 1996, Maribel appeared before the judge at the Kane County Circuit Court building, hoping it would be for the last time. Maribel was relieved that her husband wasn't there. No more veiled threats. No more looks of intimidation. She was finished with him and eager to finally end this marriage. The judge also said she would get custody of her daughter, which boosted her heart.

She was then asked to wait outside the courtroom, while the translator continued to talk to the judge inside. Maribel assumed she needed to wait for the paperwork to be completed.

While Maribel sat on a chair in the hall outside the courtroom, the translator appeared with the paperwork. Maribel looked up and reached for the white sheets of paper, then ruffled through each page, not really knowing what the words said. The translator pointed out certain sections and told her what they meant. The translator flipped through to a page where the judge presented his order. First, the marriage was declared dissolved and "forever severed." Also, Maribel was to have sole custody of their child "subject to reasonable visitation" by the father, who would be required to pay child support.

At age 25, Maribel was now a divorced woman.

Handwritten in the order was: "Plaintiff's attorney waives any attorney's fees." That was an unexpected and kind gesture by Maribel's lawyer, Patrick Kinnally.

Each page outlined the rest of the judge's orders. It was the end of her marriage, but it was also the end of broken bones, bloody lips and black eyes. It brought a newfound sense of freedom.

Maribel thought she would be excited at the final decision. Instead, tears slowly gathered in the corners of her eyes. When she married at 19, she felt it was the best possible partnership for her. He was a handsome man who was tough and feared by many in their area of Mexico. But gradually she began to fear him herself. Just hearing him come home at night was enough to stop her heart.

Now, she was finally free of him. So, why was she crying?

She was finally going to live a life without someone beating her close to death. She was not sad. Was she afraid of the unknown? Was it just relief from months and months of court dates? Time away from work? All the scheduling conflicts, lawyer meetings and paper filings? A release of stress?

Maribel felt she had lost herself, lost her personality, even lost a piece of her soul at the hands of her abusive husband. She felt trapped like an animal in a cage during her marriage. She had no life and no future. This first taste of freedom allowed her to break away from that cage and from her husband. She just needed a few minutes to absorb the newness of it all.

Yes, she would finally be able to live her life for herself and for her daughter. Maribel could now live without being beaten so badly that she would have to hide until her wounds were healed. No more broken ribs. No more stifled cries to keep Mary from hearing her pain.

Freedom.

But this freedom came at a high price. A broken family. Broken spirts. Broken self-esteem. Scars that may never completely fade away. Maybe that price will be worth it one day. Maybe she will be able to live the life she was meant to live.

But those feelings didn't last long.

A few weeks later, Maribel's ex-husband started hanging around the block where she was staying in the basement of a policewoman's home. This officer had helped her once before and just wanted to give her a hand during her time of transition after the divorce. As her ex-husband walked up and down the block, the policewoman spotted him one night and told Maribel.

"I feel bad for you, and I tried to help you with what I could. But I do not want to put my family at risk here," the officer told Maribel.

Maribel knew what that meant. The next day, she looked around to ensure her ex-husband wasn't nearby, and she started to search for another place to live. When she returned that night, her ex-husband crept up behind her as she unlocked the door. She quickly turned, this time not in fear, but with a heated defiance.

"You are still mine," he said in a hushed tone.

"No, you are not my husband anymore," Maribel said forcefully. "I am not afraid of you. Just because you give us child support that does not mean I need to accept your insults."

While he moved closer to her, Maribel pushed him away. She almost startled herself with the surge of power that flowed through her. For the first time, she was defending herself.

And just as suddenly, the threat ended. Her ex-husband stood back, surprised by Maribel's new-found strength. Perhaps, he realized he could no longer intimidate her, which was half the thrill of threatening her. He turned and ran away.

Maribel went into the house, shaking.

Another day, Maribel's ex-husband followed her to work

and cornered her again. She refused to take his abuse again and someone called the mall security. After she pulled away from him, her ex-husband ran and yelled, "You will pay for this!"

When Maribel accepted temporary shelter at a co-worker's home, the same thing happened again. Maribel's ex-husband followed her. When she was alone, he cornered her.

"You think you can run from me, but you cannot," he said. "I will always find you."

At that moment, her co-worker arrived home. Her eyes widened at seeing Maribel face-to-face with her ex-husband. He turned quickly and shot an angry look at the woman.

"You'd better get out of here," the co-worker said.

"And who are you to say that to me?" Maribel's ex-husband yelled back.

"I own this home. You are trespassing. Leave now or I will call the police."

Maribel's ex-husband slowly walked up to Maribel's co-worker.

"I will burn down your house," he said and left.

The co-worker sat down in a nearby chair and let out a long breath. She turned to Maribel and shook her head. Again, Maribel recognized that look. She had to find yet another place to live.

Soon afterward, Maribel's friend Elizabeth and her

husband made room for them. They were supportive, practical people. But after a few weeks, Elizabeth's husband took Maribel aside. He wanted to provide some consolation during this difficult time while offering words of encouragement and strength that she could stand on her own feet.

"When you first came here, you were like a little bird and your wings were broken. You just had to take some time to heal," he said. "But you are someone special, a good person. That's why you need to fly, and we understand that. You should always live by yourself. Don't live with others. If you always look for someone else to support you, you won't realize how strong you are. You can do this by yourself now. You will appreciate it better. It is the best way to be successful in your life. You can climb to the top of a mountain, but you cannot look back to see where you were. You will fall and then it will be harder to get up and start again. You just need to keep moving forward."

A few weeks later when she went to work at Marshall Field's, Maribel saw her ex-husband following her yet again. She walked up to him this time, angry and frustrated at being hounded. Maribel hesitated to call the police again. She had endured enough of the endless meetings and the paperwork and the interviews by officials. She wanted to be done with all of it, yet her ex-husband was ensuring that it was far from over.

"I'm not afraid of you anymore," Maribel yelled. She

then started yelling for help, attracting attention from other commuters and some women getting off at the nearby bus stop. Her ex-husband turned and ran again.

Coward, she thought. He was a coward all along. But not me, thought Maribel. Not anymore.

All this time, Maribel thought she was the one living in fear. Instead, he was the one who was fearful. She held her head up high and walked into the shopping mall to do her shift.

***

By spring 1997, Maribel settled into another tiny apartment in Aurora. It was adequate and quiet for the mother and daughter. But, again, her search for peace was interrupted by a bang on the door.

"Open the door," a man shouted.

"Go away," Maribel stopped, her heart skipped a beat.

The exchange continued until the man accused her of having other men inside. That's when Maribel began to shake, and Mary came out of her bedroom to stand by her mother's side. The threatening voice. The accusations. They were like flashbacks to her ex-husband. But this man was a neighbor in the apartment building, and he sounded drunk.

Maribel called Sister Ann and told her what was happening. The sister recommended that Maribel call the police. Maribel hung up. But she decided not to call the police.

Eventually, the man behind the door disappeared and all was silent again.

The next day, Maribel got a lift to church from a neighbor. When she returned to the apartment, Sister Ann and Sister Kathleen were unexpectedly on the door step and asked if she and Mary were OK. Maribel invited them inside and they sat at the kitchen table.

"When we first moved in, he seemed nice. But later he changed," Maribel said about the neighbor. "Whenever I came home from work, he would insult me. So, I ignored him."

"It's not safe for you to stay in this apartment," said Sister Kathleen.

The sisters took Maribel to see the owner of the apartment building. They sat down with him and explained the situation.

"I see," the owner said, pausing to think. "I will find a solution so this man will no longer bother you."

"That isn't good enough," said Sister Kathleen. "After all, this situation could happen again, and Maribel will be forced to call the police."

Still, the owner did not budge.

"Maribel, you signed a lease," he said, looking at Maribel. Her eyes looked down. "You are still liable for the rent for the rest of the lease."

Sister Ann turned to the owner. "If something happens to

Maribel and her daughter now, then you would be responsible," said Sister Ann.

The owner looked at the three women. He mulled over the situation and then decided to break the lease with no penalties.

Later that day, Maribel searched for yet another place to live. She soon found an apartment in another part of Aurora. This would make it easier for Mary to attend the same school and she could attend the English tutoring sessions without transportation issues.

By this time, Maribel had changed positions at Marshall Fields, leaving behind toilet cleaning for the gift wrap department. Her English improved, so she was able to converse with customers and provide better customer service.

"Although it was hard for me to talk in English, I realized I could do it," Maribel told Sister Ann during a tutoring session. "After all, I heard another woman, who could hardly speak English, and she still did an interview for a new job, and I felt I could do better."

***

By Christmas, Maribel was busy wrapping packages at the store and felt the steady stream of people would not let up. Suddenly, she saw Christina, her former counselor who had helped her, standing in the front of the line and holding a package that needed wrapping.

"Hello Maribel," Christina said.

"Christina, Merry Christmas! How are you?"

"I am good. I am so glad to see you working. Is everything ok?"

"Yes, I am doing well. I am divorced now," Maribel said in English and then paused. "What do you need? Do you want me to wrap that package?"

"Yes," Christina said, handing over a red winter coat.

The coat was heavy, and the tags dangled off the sleeves. Maribel looked over the coat and loved the red shade. She was determined to make the wrapping as beautiful as possible for her friend. So, Maribel looked for the best paper and some extra ribbon.

Christina came back in about 15 minutes to see a lushly wrapped box on the counter. Christina paid for the wrapping and then immediately handed the box back to Maribel. Confused, Maribel was about to hand it back to Christina, but stopped.

"Merry Christmas to you, Maribel. This is for you," Christina said.

Stunned, Maribel suddenly remembered all the $20 bills that Christina often slipped in her hand after her counseling sessions during those days before her divorce. This time, a lushly wrapped coat was being cradled in her arms. Maribel looked at the counselor and began to tear up.

"Merry Christmas, Maribel. It has been a pleasure to meet you," said Christina as she turned around and left the store.

Maribel felt it was more than a pleasure to meet Christina. As tough as it was after she left her ex-husband, Maribel finally realized that change was necessary to seek a better life. The counselor put her on the right path, so Maribel could learn to trust herself and her own strength while discovering that she was worthy of respect and appreciation.

Maribel also followed Christina's advice about learning English, which allowed her to gain self-confidence that would lead her to move ahead with this new life. Christina helped her to see her own gifts, and now Maribel had another gift of warmth in her hands. If only she could do that for other people, give them some gifts that would help them in their lives. Perhaps she will one day.

It wasn't long after the Christmas rush when Maribel decided to apply for a teacher's assistant position at the nearby Gates Elementary School, part of East Aurora School District 131. After all, Maribel long ago had attended the University in Mexico and had planned to work on a degree in teaching special needs students. This would be a good fit for her and would allow her to use her English skills. Sister Kathleen encouraged her to apply and even wrote a letter of recommendation for her.

Soon after Maribel submitted the application, she came

home from work with Mary, who quickly spied a blinking light on the answering machine and started to jump up and down.

"You have a message, mommy," Mary said. "Answer it!"

Maribel pressed the button to hear the principal of her daughter's school ask Maribel to come in for an interview. Maribel listened to the message five times, just to make sure she understood it. She wanted to believe it.

She excitedly called back and arranged for the job interview the next day.

After she met with the principal, she walked out with a new job.

Maribel's head swirled. It was as if a door had opened since she learned English. She jumped at the opportunity to work as a teacher's assistant. Maribel felt that getting back into a school to help students, in some way, would allow her to pay back some of the gifts she received since going on her own. It also emboldened her, making her more eager to see what else she could do. That's when she started to look for a side job, something that would help her to save more money for her future.

Maribel also began working part time on weekends in the office at the Aurora Municipal Airport. The momentum of earning more money encouraged her to work even harder. She now could put more food on the table and, more importantly, open a savings account.

***

That summer, her former father-in-law arrived in an old car to visit his granddaughter, Mary. After they greeted each other, Maribel turned toward the car and said that she, too, knew how to drive. Then the man plopped the keys into her hand and suggested they go downtown to get some ice cream for Mary.

Maribel immediately knew her bragging was a mistake. She didn't know how to drive, but she was too proud to admit otherwise and too embarrassed to make a fool of herself in front of her former father-in-law.

When she got behind the wheel, her hands shook. She silently willed herself to calm down. She then cautiously put the car into gear and slowly pulled away. The car jerked back and forth until they arrived on Lake Street. Maribel then nosed the car into a parking spot and shifted into park. She made it safely, although haphazardly, and slowly exhaled. She then gave her former father-in-law a sideways glance.

Maribel realized her father-in-law watched her closely but said little. They all left the car and went for ice cream.

After that day, the father-in-law returned every day, and asked Maribel to drive so she could get more practice. Then, right before he returned to Mexico, he handed over the keys to her.

"Keep them," he said. "You can continue to practice driving."

Maribel's heart leapt. A car. It meant more freedom, more independence and more flexibility to come and go when they wanted. No more begging rides from others. No more working around someone else's schedule. And it meant more ice cream for her darling daughter, anytime she wanted it.

Mary looked up at her mother and shrieked. "We are like eagles, mama, we can go anywhere now."

"OK, Mary, let's go to the park. We are eagles now," said Maribel.

***

While Maribel always watched her friends as they drove, she longed to do the same with confidence. She avidly watched how they easily handled the steering wheel, how they turned the car, and how they moved their right leg from the gas pedal to the brake pedal. That's when her friends encouraged her to learn the proper way to drive.

Victor, a friend from a church she once attended, agreed to help Maribel learn how to drive so she could take the test for a driver's license.

They first met at the church's parking lot on a Saturday afternoon, but soon moved to an empty lot at a nearby old factory where Maribel practiced driving to her heart's content. Eventually, she learned even the most basic how-to steps: fill the gas tank with gasoline, check the oil level, check the tire pressure and even fix a flat tire.

When her former father-in-law came to visit again, he took Maribel for her driver's license test. Maribel was nervous, but she hid her fear. The tester seemed rude once he got into her car and challenged her to turn right and then left. When she returned to the testing facility, she asked to speak to a manager and said her tester was too rude and requested another person. While she waited a few hours, she finally got a new tester, who later said she needed to practice going in reverse before she could get her license. Maribel was dejected.

At the same time, she was eager to prove she could do this.

Maribel returned a week later. The tester remembered her and said she returned too soon. So, she asked for someone else. Another tester went with her in the car. After some routine moves, he told her to return to the facility.

"You passed," the tester said.

"Are you sure?" said Maribel, surprised.

"What? You want to do more?" he said.

"No! I'm good, thank you!"

Maribel felt relieved. She finally had a driver's license.

Chapter 14

JUANITA FINDS A NEW PATH TO LEARN

Over the next three years at the center, Juanita grew stronger emotionally, mentally and spiritually. She did not realize how those other parts of herself needed to grow with her. But they finally did and she felt like she was catching up to where she needed to be in life. She had more confidence. She had more energy to do everyday tasks because she had a better grasp of the English language and could converse with people anywhere. She smiled now at others who passed by, despite how her father used to caution her that it could be dangerous to be friendly to strangers. It was safer to be isolated.

Not anymore.

"Yes, you can do it," Sister Kathleen said to Juanita when she shied away from even grocery shopping by herself.

Sister Kathleen would never say, "No." She always said, "You can do it" or "You'll be OK."

That meant the world to Juanita.

Those words in English gave her the courage to go to the grocery store or shopping mall, to the doctor with her children and even to an automated teller machine (ATM). She could buy something and, if need be, she could return it by herself without her husband. In fact, that was one of her biggest tests. A while ago, Juanita brought home a new dress and found that it did not fit. She then asked Jaime to return it for her.

"You can return it yourself," Jaime said, gently, hoping to nudge Juanita into taking control of the situation.

Juanita felt a stab of fear. At first, she was surprised to hear Jaime say that. But she realized, again, it was time that she took care of these things by herself. She gathered her strength, got into the car and drove to the store. Shaking, she walked into the store and up to a cashier. While she hesitated at first, she then spoke in English that she wanted to return a dress.

The cashier began the transaction. Just like that.

Juanita's heart stopped racing. Her fears cooled as she looked at the cashier. The woman understood Juanita's English.

After the transaction for the return was completed, the cashier gave Juanita a receipt and she walked out of the store with one of the biggest smiles she ever had. Juanita said what she wanted — in English and in public — and she was understood. She felt like she had graduated, in a way. She saw a new chapter opening.

When Juanita returned home, Jaime embraced his wife as soon as she entered the front door. He was proud that she went by herself to handle something she needed to do. Her dependence and her insecurities were waning, and Jaime knew Juanita was standing on her own two feet again.

"Congratulations," Jaime said to Juanita. "Now, that didn't hurt, did it?"

"No," Juanita said. "No, it didn't. It felt good."

While she had a sense of independence in Mexico, she had somehow lost it when she moved to the United States. Now, she slowly regained it on American soil. In some ways, Juanita was transforming into herself again, only different and new. Besides Jaime, Juanita also credited Sister Kathleen with helping her to do more and to be more of a woman who could now go out into that world.

Juanita also started helping others with learning the English language.

"I saw someone at the store trying to explain what they wanted," Juanita told Jaime one night. "I offered to help her and she said, 'Yes.' If she had said, 'No,' then I would not have helped. But I was able to help her."

After all, Juanita knew what it was like to feel lost and isolated in a new place. She wanted to make sure people knew others were kind and helpful and they were not alone.

Chapter 15

BLANCA IS EAGER TO ADVANCE

In 1993, Blanca had her eye on the top supervisor's position for housekeeping at the medical center. She was eager to work her way up after being a housekeeper and had picked up some English here and there. But it was not good enough to advance her further in a career.

She knew she had to put more effort into learning English, not only to speak it, but to read and write it as well. She also lacked a General Education Diploma, or GED, which was needed to advance. She needed to take more steps to improve her education, which would help her achieve that GED. Then she could be taken as a serious candidate for the top supervisory role, which would lead to more money and a chance to prove her skills.

Then she learned about the sisters at the Dominican Literacy Center in Aurora. They were helping immigrants like herself to learn or to improve their English skills. She decided to see Sister Kathleen about starting the tutoring sessions. The sooner she mastered English, the sooner she could get that promotion and earn more money for her family.

Blanca told Sister Kathleen that she needed to improve her English so she could eventually earn the GED, which was necessary if she was going to get any promotions. After she registered at the center, Blanca worked on her English during the tutoring sessions twice a week with Sister Kathleen. Blanca also knew Juanita Rodriguez, who attended the literacy center, because they both worked at the medical center.

Blanca paid a babysitter to watch her children so she could attend the English sessions in the morning and then she worked her second shift job, from 4 p.m. to midnight. Sometimes, she brought the kids to the center or her husband helped by watching them. She worked closely with Sister Kathleen as they went through the workbooks, page by page.

While Blanca learned English during the tutoring sessions face-to-face, she sometimes found it harder to understand someone who was speaking English on the telephone. Eventually, she trained herself to overcome that. When she wasn't at the tutoring sessions at the center, she was doing homework while her children slept.

Once Blanca finished her English sessions at the center,

she earned a certificate. But that was just the first step. Now, she tackled classes to earn her GED as Sister Kathleen offered extra guidance in math and algebra. Blanca felt driven, eager to fit in the extra help and finally earning the GED, all while taking care of her family.

Chapter 16

TERESA SETS FOUR GOALS

A year already passed since Teresa and her children moved to Aurora to be with Miguel, and they settled into a mobile home. During this time, another son, Lazaro, was born.

Although she was busy raising their children, Teresa set four goals for herself: She wanted to get a green card and establish permanent residency in the United States. She wanted to learn to drive and get a driver's license. She also wanted to become a U.S. citizen. And most of all, she wanted to learn how to speak English and become a part of society.

In 1995, Teresa got a chance at one of those dreams. She was attending Mass at her church when a friend there told her that some religious sisters taught English at the nearby Dominican Literacy Center. Teresa decided to register at the center, as if she was about to sow seeds of knowledge, instead of seeds on a farm.

When Teresa heard about the center, it pumped new life into her. She felt she was ready to learn English, especially since it would give her a new way to connect with others at church and in her neighborhood.

Before coming to the center, she was always told that she did not have much education and lacked a good foundation to learn the language. Despite those drawbacks, she was determined to speak English.

***

At the center, Teresa quickly registered and was then assigned a tutor named Judy. They began to work with simple words to learn their meaning. Soon, Teresa moved on to English words for numbers, colors, fruits and other objects.

Teresa felt like she got a new lifeline while working with Judy. It offered her a chance to ask questions immediately when she didn't understand something. She made mistakes, but that didn't matter because it was just between the two of them. It allowed her to learn and she became proud of her accomplishment. The more she learned, the more her confidence was fueled.

Slowly, she learned and understood what she was saying in English, especially as she mastered simple sentences.

During that time, the sisters from the center visited Teresa and her family at their home on Thanksgiving and again on

Christmas, bringing donated food and clothes and a few toys for her children. Teresa was touched by the kindness of the sisters and felt the gifts arrived at the right time because she was so short of money during the holidays. Teresa felt that God put the sisters there, like angels, to help her.

Chapter 17

MARIA FINDS HER NICHE

Maria and Valentin stayed in their one-bedroom home for about nine years before deciding to buy a bigger house. This time, they selected a two-level frame home with three bedrooms. It was a better-quality home and Maria definitely felt they were moving up in society, despite a bigger mortgage and more maintenance bills. They just worked harder to save more money, despite going without some things for themselves.

Maria also took another big step. She signed up for an English as a Second Language class at nearby Waubonsee Community College. While some students laughed at her for making the wrong choices of words, she also became intimidated by the peer pressure. The other students already knew more English compared to her few meager words. And too often, Maria didn't understand what the teacher was saying.

Dejected, she eventually stopped going to the class.

***

In 1998, Maria heard from some people about the Dominican Literacy Center. They said the Catholic sisters, who taught at the center, did not embarrass anyone as they tried to learn English. This had to be the right path that Maria needed to learn English and to take hold of her future. She quickly arranged to meet the sisters.

When Maria started the English tutoring sessions, she was shy and nervous and wondered how she would be treated. But her tutor, Sister Ann, always had a smile when she greeted Maria at the front door. The atmosphere of friendliness and peace was striking. Maria couldn't believe it. Was this really happening? She felt it was good luck finding a place with such kindness … and she knew that she would learn English.

Sister Ann was patient when Maria came two days a week for the tutoring sessions and studied as hard as she could. Maria found that the one-on-one sessions helped her to better learn and understand the language and she quickly picked up the lessons each time. She knew that once she mastered English, she would have a future where doors would open, instead of doors that closed to her as a youngster. This time, she did not have anyone or anything stopping her from an education.

Maria also experienced something different: peace and encouragement without peer pressure.

Most of all, Sister Ann saw promise in Maria, because she

was a good student and learned quickly. To help Maria pick up English even more, Sister Ann asked what she enjoyed.

"History. I like history. I also like to learn about Thanksgiving and other holidays," Maria said.

At the next session, Sister Ann opened some history books related to Thanksgiving and they read them in English. Maria would occasionally ask a question and Sister Ann answered. Most of all, Sister Ann asked Maria questions about what she just read to make sure she understood it in English.

Maria often brought her son, Alonzo, to the tutoring sessions and marveled at how Sister Ann would sit on the floor and play with him or give him some toys to keep him occupied for the rest of the lessons.

In fact, when Alonzo started kindergarten, he tested right into the English-speaking classes. Maria wondered how that was possible, how was Alonzo able to speak better English than his own mother? The tester at school asked Alonzo and he said, "Because of my mom's classes." He was listening during each of Maria's English tutoring sessions with Sister Ann and quickly picked up the words while playing in the background. Ironically, Alonzo needed some Spanish lessons to communicate with his older family members, including his grandmother, whenever she visited them from Mexico.

Once she became proficient in English, Maria was able to

read and to understand the street signs. This encouraged Maria to drive the car more and take it further than she typically did before, instead of limiting herself. She even started driving her children to the doctor without her husband. He no longer needed to take time off from his job or lose any wages just to be her translator. And it was all happening since she learned English.

Chapter 18

THE CENTER EXPANDS

Besides the daytime tutoring sessions, the center soon offered a small class at night. By June 1994, Sister Kathleen anticipated more growth and knew that she needed to find a larger, more permanent home for the center. She began looking at buildings in the northeast quadrant of Aurora, a poor neighborhood where many immigrants lived. None of the buildings that she saw were a good fit. Then she heard that St. Therese's Convent on Vermont Street was empty. The religious sisters who lived there had long since retired from teaching at St. Therese's school and the parish wanted to rent the building.

When Sister Kathleen saw the 17-room building, it felt perfect. The small rooms, all former bedrooms for sisters, would be good, comfortable spots for tutor-student pairs during their lessons. When she spoke to the pastor, Father Gerald Paul, he wanted to rent the building as a residence. But after listening to Sister Kathleen's plan, he agreed to rent to the Dominicans for the new literacy center. He knew the need for this type of program was great, and he wanted the parish to support it.

Sister Kathleen also boosted the center's staff. She enlisted Sister Virginia Derhake as a tutor. Sister Ann, who was a volunteer tutor, became a coordinator for the tutoring program, which continued to increase. Sister Ann loved the work. She loved the students and loved getting to know their families. She loved everything that she did. And it showed.

One of Sister Ann's students was Francesca. While they started with the alphabet in English, Francesca eventually learned enough so she could advance from her green card and permanent residency to U.S. citizenship. Sister Ann also taught another woman, who was a dentist in Mexico, but she could not use her license in Illinois. She, too, sought to learn English to gain a foothold in the community.

Sister Ann had yet another student, who wanted to learn English to better understand the meaning of the terms "weekly," "monthly" and "quarterly." Sister Ann later learned that the woman, who was a housekeeper, was doing everything she was assigned at one time, instead of knowing that some tasks were meant to be done only at certain times. Sister Ann then developed an index card system with English words for her duties on one side and the Spanish translation on the other side. So, when the supervisor pointed at the card with her task, the woman would know what duties to perform and when. The cards worked well until her English became more fluent.

***

In 1996, Sister Judith opened the second Dominican Literacy Center at Our Lady of Grace Parish in the Logan Square neighborhood of Chicago, at the request of the pastor, Father Thomas Tivy. It operated as a separate educational unit from the Aurora center and, after receiving a start-up grant through the Aurora center, sought its own funding. Sister Kathleen also donated computers and materials to get the new center started.

This time, it was up to Sister Judith to develop the second center's revenue streams to keep it viable. So, she diligently researched state and other programs. When funding was secured, the center started with about 15 students and two tutors during its first year.

One of Sister Judith's first students had a son with cancer who was in the hospital. While the hospital had a bilingual staff, they were not available after regular business hours. And it was during those later hours when the woman found it difficult to communicate with the second shift health care professionals about her son. That's when she decided to come to the Dominican Literacy Center. She had one goal in mind — to learn English so she could know fully about her son's health. The mother learned English and then listened intently to the doctors and nurses. Eventually, the boy's cancer went into remission.

After about 12 years, the Logan Square center continued to grow with both volunteers and students. But the building also had an increasing need for costly repairs. Instead of pouring more money into the old building, the sisters decided to move the literacy center.

In 2008, the second center re-opened on the second floor of a former Franciscan convent in Melrose Park, Illinois, that was rented from Sacred Heart Catholic Parish. It still had the stained-glass windows of the chapel, which was now turned into the center's library with some computers loaded with Rosetta Stone language software. Students were able to use the translation software by speaking loudly, so the software would catch their words.

Sister Judith also was learning a lot about the Hispanic culture during the tutoring sessions. She heard first-hand how the women courageously left behind their countries, their families and their friends to settle in the United States. All were seeking a better job, a safer environment and a better life. The women were hard-working, typically seeking laborious jobs to make money, and then they would send that money back to their families in their home countries. They remained family oriented, even with such distances between them. While here in the United States, they wanted to learn English so they could find a job, or obtain a better job or a promotion, to understand their children and to help them with their homework.

One woman, who worked as a secretary at an elementary school, asked to be a volunteer tutor after she went to a courtroom to watch a trial where a boy was accused of a crime. The boy didn't speak English and didn't understand anything going on in the courtroom. That inspired the woman to want to teach others how to speak English. Sister Judith asked the new tutor what happened in the courtroom.

"That boy was charged with shooting and killing my daughter," the tutor said. "She was my only child. I felt becoming a tutor was a way of forgiving."

Sister Judith was moved by the woman's words. She found such stories enhanced her perspective in dealing with others. Every person was valuable to know. She felt it was a privilege to work with both the students and the tutors. Sister Judith, who had spent 30 years as a teacher or as an administrator, had never thought of tutoring adults until she headed this new literacy center. Since, then, she loved every minute of it.

Sister Judith was later joined by Sister Beverly Jeanne Howe as an assistant director. Sister Beverly also focused on pastoral work and canon law in Rockford, Illinois. She accepted Sister Judith's offer to assist after caring for her ailing mother, who later had died.

Sister Beverly came with no expectations. She wanted to help in any way she could. The sisters had no reservations of what it was like to interface with someone who didn't understand English. That's how her skills over a lifetime helped at the center.

While the Melrose Park center was getting established, the Dominican Literacy Center in Aurora in 1998 started a new program for immigrants seeking to pass the U.S. citizenship test, led by Sister Jane Ann Beckman. And the student ranks at both locations continued to grow.

**

Kathie Walsh, a retired doctor, was a volunteer tutor on Sister Judith's team and moved with the center from Logan Square to Melrose Park. She had been in private family practice for about 30 years and affiliated with West Suburban Hospital in Oak Park, Illinois. She also enjoyed being a director of the residency program of family medicine at the hospital for about six years and taught at the Loyola University Stritch School of Medicine.

Her extensive work was the reason that she received the Loyola University Stritch School of Medicine's Stritch Medal, the highest honor for inspiring leadership, contributions to medical education and a tireless commitment to compassionate patient-centered care. Her medical career was fulfilling, mostly because she strongly believed it was important to help people from cradle to grave.

Yet as she prepared to retire, Kathie did not want to slow down as many people tend to do at this stage of life. An inner drive and a need to continue to help people compelled her to seek some type of fulfilling volunteer work.

That opportunity came in 2008, when she picked up the bulletin at Ascension Catholic Church in Oak Park after Mass on a Sunday morning. Her eyes caught an ad that sought volunteer tutors at the Dominican Literacy Center in Logan Square, which wasn't far from her new home in suburban River Forest, which bordered Oak Park, known as the birthplace of legendary writer, Ernest Hemingway.

Kathie was familiar with the Dominican Sisters. She was taught by Dominicans while going through high school at Our Lady of the Elms in Akron, Ohio, where she grew up. That connection spurred her interest. But could she picture herself as a tutor of English as a second language? She liked the concept of working with women, one-on-one, and not standing in front of a classroom or lecturing. But she never served as a tutor before. While the program offered training, it seemed daunting. Still, volunteer tutors received 16 hours of initial instruction and ongoing in-service training, so it provided a good foundation. Kathie decided to try it.

She met with Sister Judith, who told her about the program and the women who participated. As a tutor, Kathie would have to commit to at least one-and-a-half hours per week to her student. Kathie returned home and thought about the chance to assist someone seeking to learn English. Helping someone to achieve that goal was quite an incentive. Would Kathie help to open doors for them? Would these students then go on to do good things in the community?

Kathie wanted to do it, since it would give her an opportunity to help someone else. It also would allow her flexibility to still teach at Loyola's medical school and help her husband, Joseph, an ordained deacon in the Catholic church who was undergoing treatments for cancer.

Kathie intently listened to Sister Judith during her training sessions, soaking up all the details she needed to help her first student, Paula.

At the beginning, Kathie questioned how successful she might be as a tutor. The most important part was to get to know Paula. But Paula knew very little English when they first met. It would be difficult to ask how her day was or even what her favorite color was. Still, Kathie felt a commitment from Paula, who was receiving some assistance from her twin sons and her husband.

At first, Paula was hesitant to open up. But as their one-on-one sessions continued, they each began to share more. Eventually, a bond of trust developed between the two women.

"Take a chance and talk. Don't be shy. No one will embarrass you," Kathie encouraged Paula.

Paula sounded out the words and soon began putting together sentences in English. She never missed a session and started enjoying the use of flash cards as well as lessons with the language software.

Eventually, their relationship as tutor and student grew. Paula even invited Kathie to her twin sons' First Communion. Kathie was happy to attend and enjoyed the party afterward with the mariachi band and a table filled with a variety of foods. This event allowed Kathie to see Paula as more than just a student. It opened up Kathie's own world and how she understood language and how it was used. It also helped Kathie grow as a tutor. With each succeeding lesson, Kathie's confidence in tutoring improved, especially when she saw her student's progress.

As Paula's English improved, Kathie started her sessions with a 10- to 15-minute conversation in English. Then they spent time on the workbooks, Rosetta Stone, flash cards and magazines. Kathie also encouraged Paula to use the center's library and weekly book discussions.

Volunteering at the center helped to build Kathie's respect

for another culture and its people. They worked hard. They were committed to learning English. They were committed to family.

The volunteer work also gave Kathie a sense of fulfillment. It helped her during a time that would become more disheartening as Joseph continued with an endless stream of medical appointments and chemo sessions.

As the months passed, Kathie juggled teaching and her volunteer work at the center while helping Joseph. The long waits for doctor appointments and test results were agonizing. Eventually, Joseph had surgery, but it did not produce the results they had hoped. So, they trudged through more doctor visits and treatments.

As time passed, Kathie hired a caregiver, since Joseph needed more assistance every day. Kathie even trimmed back her schedule to ensure more time with Joseph and worked alongside the caregiver, when needed. Their two sons, two daughters and nine grandchildren also took turns visiting whenever they could.

While Kathie fielded appointments for Joseph, she continued providing tutoring lessons for Paula. As Kathie watched her student progress, Paula became more assertive and spoke English with more confidence. She held conversations in English. Her comprehension was good. And the metamorphosis helped her to develop more leadership skills. Paula soon found herself being a spokeswoman for the literacy center by passing the word of her own transformation to others who could benefit.

After Paula finished her three-year program at the center, she became more fluent in English and decided to become more active in her children's school. She eventually became a vice president of the Parent Teacher Organization (PTO). Learning English was the key to accomplishing many things in society, Paula found, especially while getting involved in local school issues.

By early 2016, Kathie's husband was becoming weaker. They did not rent a hospital bed for him because Kathie wanted to keep things as normal as possible, all while the children and grandchildren spent more time with him. Eucharistic ministers also came to the house to serve Communion to Joseph, who could only nod his acceptance of the Body of Christ. During those visits, the ministers also selected some readings from the New Testament or recited some prayers as Joseph and Kathie followed. But soon that became too taxing for Joseph.

Kathie watched as her husband's health continued to deteriorate until he passed away in March 2016. That's when Kathie, full of grief and tired from the long battle alongside her husband, took a couple of weeks off from tutoring at the center to handle the funeral arrangements and, later, Joseph's estate matters.

She now found herself soaking up every minute with her

family, who lingered long after the funeral, wanting to know if she needed anything more. While Kathie cherished her time with her family, she needed to learn how to cherish who she was now. A widow. Now, it was time for herself. She needed to be alone to finally realize what life would be like without Joseph and to rediscover herself.

Eventually, Kathie returned to her regular schedule of volunteer work and teaching. It became more meaningful to her now, and it helped her to cope with the grief. It also continued to develop her own legacy of learning by allowing her to return to helping people achieve their dreams at the literacy center.

After Paula, another of Kathie's students won an award for her parish activities. Still another became more active in her church choir. Others got jobs babysitting or at restaurants or other nearby businesses. They earned money, started savings accounts, paid their bills and fulfilled wishes with their families that they didn't think were possible before learning English.

While their lives improved, so did Kathie's. It gave new meaning to her life while she, in turn, gained a gift of learning something from each student.

***

By 2008, the Aurora center faced a major challenge at a time when immigration became a polarizing topic in many circles and anti-immigration rhetoric was gaining momentum.

The flow of new immigrants into the area around the literacy center began to slow, compared to the influx Sister Kathleen had seen in the early 1990s when the center started.

The Great Recession was taking hold, and many homeowners in Aurora and nationwide faced foreclosures of their condos, single-family homes and townhomes. Wave after wave of foreclosures hit the Chicago region as short sales were posted by whipsawed owners hoping to wrangle what little value was left of their homes. Many were losing their homes because of job losses, overwhelming medical bills or credit card debt. They tried desperately to stall their losses.

While many homes were under water and some area businesses closed their doors, Sister Kathleen and her staff hunkered down to keep the Dominican Literacy Center's doors open, especially now that it was serving a variety of immigrant students from several countries around the world. Her staff of paid employees and volunteers continued to grow exponentially to fit the needs of the center's student population. Luckily, she had organized an advisory board back in 1995 and was advised to save whatever surplus money they had at the end of each school year. She reinvested the surplus, which grew into a substantial emergency fund.

As the Great Recession held a tight grip, that emergency fund came in handy. After all, many grants and donations were reduced or even stopped, which forced the center to tighten its belt. While the center did not lay off any staff, Sister Kathleen was forced to dip into the emergency fund and, ultimately, withdraw about 25 percent to keep the center's budget intact. The experience led them to start a "Sponsor a Student" donation program, which also helped to keep the center afloat.

Since then, the center garnered about $220,000 in grants and funding. Donors included The Alfred Bersted Foundation, the Dollar General Foundation, the Chicago Tribune/McCormick Fund, the Dunham Fund, the Illinois Secretary of State Literacy Office and the Westerman Foundation, along with many individual donations. The center, thankfully, stayed open as more immigrants continued to register. Alison Brzyzinski then became the new tutoring coordinator in 2014 when Sister Ann moved to Springfield to take care of her aging father.

The Dominican Literacy Center set the cost for each student at $125. About $100 was covered by donations, while the remaining $25 was paid by the student to cover books and materials. Sister Kathleen asked students to bring some small things, like napkins, cups and even treats, such as cookies or cake, to share with their fellow students during the tutoring year from September through June. It was a way for them to contribute to their diverse micro-community of students and to extend good will to each other. Whatever their country of origin, Sister Kathleen never asked incoming students about their citizenship status. It did not matter. The doors were open to all.

"We are all learning and contributing," Sister Kathleen said to one student. "We are living in a community and we are all learning from each other."

By the end of the school year, the students pitched in together to clean the school, from top to bottom, using donated cleaning supplies, or some that were bought at the local dollar store. Doing the work as a team got the job done quickly and the building was ready for the fall, signifying a fresh start.

After students finished the tutoring programs, they could sign up for English conversation classes or they could consider becoming U.S. citizens. The citizenship class semesters started in February and September and ran for 12 weeks each. Usually, 20 students signed up for the morning sessions and about 30 students in the evening classes.

Immigration and deportation issues were heating up nationwide and were evident in Aurora as the center's classes continued to increase. After these students applied to the government, they lived as permanent residents and contributed to society. Then, they could take the U.S. citizenship classes to prepare for the citizenship test and, finally, take the oath.

"This is like a vocation within a vocation," thought Sister Kathleen of her work at the center.

While she had loved being a teacher and a principal, including at St. Bernadette School in Evergreen Park, Illinois, the Dominican Literacy Center was different. She often found that these immigrant women were transparent and open, especially to the community.

"This experience makes me grateful for what I have," Sister Kathleen thought. "These immigrants believe it is first God, then their family. It's easy for us to forget that."

PART 4
SOARING ABOVE THE CLOUDS

Chapter 19

MARIBEL FINISHES THE COURSE

On a soft spring day in 1999, Maribel was nervous as she walked into the Dominican Literacy Center, more so than on the first day when she arrived. Today, she was not going to have a regular tutoring session. The workbooks were now finished and closed. The magazines were returned to the racks.

Instead, Sister Ann took Maribel to a nearby café for her so-called graduation. She wanted Maribel to decide what she wanted to eat and then order her meal by speaking in English.

Maribel was nervous while she looked over the menu. She eventually decided and ordered coffee and a sandwich. They ate quietly, while Maribel looked around. She finally realized what it was like to go into any restaurant in the United States and order a meal, all while speaking English. In some ways, it was more than a graduation, of sorts. It was a moment of liberation — a chance to finally begin fitting into American society.

Later, when they returned to the center, Maribel felt emboldened and took the momentous occasion a step further. She sat down with both Sister Ann and Sister Kathleen.

"I plan to buy a house," Maribel said.

Maribel was tired of moving from someone's basement to yet another apartment. It was time to settle down and give Mary a stable home.

Maribel saw the sisters look at each other and she suddenly looked down, wondering if she overstepped in some way. Sister Ann said buying a house was a serious endeavor and it depended on how much income the buyer made, how much money they could afford as a down-payment and how much she could pay in monthly mortgage payments. Then, there were the monthly utility bills and maintenance costs.

Maribel outlined her finances. She knew it would be very tight. Yet she was determined, just like she was the day she decided to move forward with her divorce. It was a chance to open another new door.

This time, that open door was going to be the door to her own home. She was ready. Even if her finances weren't.

***

After she finished her English lessons at the Dominican Literacy Center, Maribel decided to enter Waubonsee Community College to further improve her English and registered for an English as a Second Language class.

One afternoon, she sat in her car in the parking lot after class and organized some papers. The passenger side door suddenly opened and Maribel's ex-husband slid in beside her.

Startled, Maribel couldn't believe her eyes. She was finally getting on her feet and starting to heal from his cruelty. It was clear he had been stalking her for some time, since he knew when she left her class and went to her car. He did this despite moving on in his life with another woman and having a child with her.

A chill ran down Maribel's spine.

He sat quietly for a second, as if collecting his thoughts, while Maribel's anger bubbled to the surface.

"What are you doing here?" she hissed.

"I am going back to Mexico. I want you to come with me," he said quietly.

"No. NO!" Maribel said firmly. "You have a second chance at a family. You have another child now. And you're going to ruin that, too."

With that, Maribel's ex-husband barreled out of the car and slammed the door.

That was the last time Maribel saw him.

It was also when Maribel decided to delay advancing her English skills and left behind her classes at Waubonsee.

***

When her father-in-law returned to Aurora, Maribel felt it was only fair to return the car that he left with her. With some savings along with an additional $125 in borrowed money, she put a down payment on a used red Nissan. She loved it, mostly because it was her car. It gave her a new and deeper sense of freedom every time she got behind the wheel and turned on the engine. It revved up, like her heart, into a rush of freedom like she had never experienced before. It also allowed her to get to work on time and not worry about bus schedules and bad weather delays.

One night, when she came home from work, she saw some cars pull up across the street, including a white car. By the time she reached the back door, a man appeared behind her. She quickly pulled the screen door in front of her for protection, then pushed the door toward the man to shove him away. But the man kept saying they were friends and pressed against the door.

"Go away. LEAVE!" Maribel yelled.

Suddenly, the man pulled a long ice pick from behind his back and thrust it at her, striking a Bible she held in her arm. He also attempted to drag her to his car as she pleaded with him to stop and screamed. For the second time in her life, Maribel felt she was going to die. She screamed for Lupita, the owner of the home where she was now renting a room upstairs.

The man dropped her and ran to his car. Maribel ran to a neighbor's house, yelling, "He's going to kill me."

Her neighbor opened her door and they called the police. When the police arrived, they searched the immediate area unsuccessfully and left without the assailant. Maribel shivered with fear and could not sleep that night. She sat up, watching the street through her window. She then saw the same white car circle the block a number of times. She sat in the chair all night, strategically keeping the phone nearby ... and a knife in her hand.

By 5:30 a.m., Maribel was still afraid and called a friend from church to watch her daughter and to keep her away from the house for a while. Maribel then went to work.

Two weeks later, Maribel saw the same man again when they pulled up, side by side, at a stoplight. He began to laugh. She reported the incident to the police, but an officer said nothing could be done without a license plate number or the name of the man.

A few days later, when Maribel was driving, a car ran a red light and hit her Nissan. Her car was badly damaged, and the insurance would not pay for the car. Her car, her symbol of freedom, was totaled. Yet she had to continue making payments because she still owed money on the loan.

Resourceful, Maribel either arranged to get rides from

others or borrowed a car to get to where she needed to be. Nothing was going to stop her from working and making money to support her daughter.

Whatever happened in Maribel's life, she always kept going. Something inside of her propelled her forward. She did not want to quit. She wanted to set a good example for her daughter. She also never wanted to date and expose her to any other men. She was finished with that.

***

By 2000, Maribel had been enjoying a job at a manufacturing plant, where she was making more money than she had ever anticipated. She was able to easily pay her bills, to continue to save and to provide a good life for herself and for Mary.

She also began enjoying herself and making friends. One of those friends invited her over for coffee, but never expected it to lead to a new kind of commitment. Her friend, Edith, was divorced just like Maribel, so they felt a kinship. There were other women there like her, single again and surviving.

When she entered Edith's condo, Maribel was in awe of what Edith could afford. The condo was light and airy and well decorated. It felt like a home should feel.

"Why don't you buy one?" Edith said.

"Oh, I don't know," Maribel said. "I wouldn't know how to do it."

"It's a long process, but a great Realtor could help you with that," she said.

Another friend quickly recommended a Realtor and Maribel scribbled down the name, as the women continued to chat for the rest of the afternoon.

That night, Maribel mulled over whether to call the Realtor. Mary was in middle school now and she was concerned about uprooting her again, unless they could stay within the school district. She also had a secure job and had saved enough money for a condo or a modest townhouse, which felt safer than a single-family home. So, she made the call and decided to start a search for her own home, a place that could help to shape her future.

After checking on a number of locations, Maribel had a passing interest in one townhome. But when the Realtor opened the door to a third-floor condo, Maribel held her breath. It felt like home. Sure, there were some older appliances and the worn carpet had to be replaced. But Maribel looked beyond that. It felt safe.

Now, Maribel was torn. Mary liked a townhome they saw earlier, mostly because it had a basement, where she could play and dream. But Maribel could more easily afford the condo. How could she disappoint her daughter, yet how could she struggle again just to live day by day and worry about paying bills?

That night, Maribel sat down with Mary and asked which new home she wanted.

"The townhome! It has a basement and I could play down there," Mary said.

"But then, I won't see you anymore," said Maribel. "If I buy the townhome, I will need to get a second job to pay for it."

Mary sat silently for a minute, thinking about her mother being gone for most of the day versus her own playtime.

"We don't need more space," said Mary. "It's just the two of us. We can get the condo."

The next day, Maribel arranged to see the condo again and put in her offer. Two days later, she discovered a couple also had put in an offer. The Realtor reassured Maribel that they just need to wait and see if the couple's offer was accepted.

Then, during a visit with her friend Betty, they immediately wanted to talk about her house hunting.

"We placed an offer, but now the place is probably gone," said Maribel, explaining about the competing offer on the same condo.

Betty's husband, Arthur, came out and asked what was going on and he shook his head, knowing his friend wanted a good home where she could feel safe.

"Do you believe in the Lord?" said Arthur.

"Yes," Maribel quickly said.

"Then, pray for the house."

The three then paused, lowered their heads, closed their eyes and prayed together.

After Maribel left her friends and entered the door to her apartment that night, the phone rang. It was the Realtor. Maribel nervously picked up the phone, eager to hear which offer was accepted for the condo.

Stunned, Maribel heard the words "your offer was accepted" and continued to listen to the Realtor explain about the next steps they needed to take to secure the sale.

She and her daughter would finally be a part of the American dream. A good job. A good home. Food on the table. Food that she bought and cooked and served. No more stale bagels from a trash can or stretching a lone cookie between the two of them when her cabinets were bare. This house was going to be a home where she could raise her daughter and grow old.

When the sale closed and Maribel received the keys, she looked at them like they were precious pieces of gold. She drove to the condo, went to her front door, and nervously inserted the key. The lock clicked and opened, and they finally entered a whole new era of their lives. Mary did not immediately see that milestone, instead she began jumping and running from room to room.

"It's a palace!" said Mary, shrieking with joy. "We can do

what we want now. No one will say anything to us. We don't have to move again!"

The condo was not far from the Marshall Field's, where Maribel used to work. Whenever she took the bus during those years, she would pass by this condominium complex and often thought to herself, "God, I would love to live there."

She finally arrived.

Maribel walked around the empty condo, this time as the owner, and felt a new strength growing within her. She now felt it was possible to make plans for a more secure future. So, she eyed each room with a vision for when it would be totally transformed into her own. She intended to put flowers and plants and even a small table on the balcony, so that she and Mary could have breakfast outside.

Most of all, the condo was more than just a place to live. It meant safety and security and a chance to fulfill her dreams. Maribel paused as she stood on the balcony. She then looked at the sky.

"Thank you, God, for giving us this place to live," she said in a silent prayer.

Little by little, Maribel started to move into the condo. She bought new carpeting, painted the walls and changed the kitchen floor tiles. While she transformed the condo, the condo was beginning to transform her.

***

As Maribel settled into her condo, she also faced new challenges at work. She was promoted to manager at the manufacturing plant and began to supervise several workers.

With each good review and raise that she earned, her morale was boosted further. The more she was complimented, the harder she worked. There were other immigrants like her at the plant, so she felt a sense of camaraderie. But she also wanted to differentiate herself and improve her presentation of the English language so she would be taken more seriously by those who were not immigrants.

After she learned the basics of the English language at the Dominican Literacy Center, she registered again at Waubonsee Community College for English as a Second Language. This time, she was committed to perfecting her sentence structure, pronunciation and presentation, so she could clearly communicate with her peers and those she supervised. She did not want to hear any potential snide remarks that someone couldn't understand her accent or that her English structure wasn't good.

She attended the classes, studied at home and ensured that she got as much as she could from each session. She was determined to be fluent and to communicate with ease.

By 2009, Maribel completed her coursework and was chosen to be one of the speakers at a special ceremony at

Waubonsee where she would receive her certificate. She was nervous yet exhilarated at the idea of public speaking for the first time. So many thoughts rushed through her mind about what to say. There was so much she wanted to express for a day she did not expect to see.

Before she left the condo for her milestone ceremony, she glanced again at her carefully crafted speech that outlined her thoughts about completing the coursework and what it meant for her and her daughter after escaping her abusive husband, getting an order of protection, going through divorce proceedings and stopping him from stalking her again and again. She also stepped up and away from those early days of being a single mother in poverty and near starvation. No more stale bagels from a garbage can liner behind a retail store. No more minimum wage.

Now, after being told for years that she was not good at anything, she was earning a certificate in the English language. She believed it would help her to do even more in life.

She rushed by a steady stream of students in the hallway at Waubonsee and made her way to the auditorium for the ceremony. Just then, Maribel ran into Sister Kathleen and Sister Ann.

Surprised at the coincidence, they immediately hugged each other as the sisters smiled, the same welcoming smile they offered when Maribel first met them on the threshold of the center. That spot literally became the threshold of her new life. The sisters then mentioned how they just watched another former student who graduated, and they were just about to leave the campus.

"Could you stay? I am speaking at the ESL ceremony in a few minutes. I would love to have you there," Maribel said.

The sisters looked at each other, checked their watches to ensure they could be back at the center in time for other commitments and agreed to sit in the audience. Maribel was thrilled. Besides the ESL certificate, she also was receiving a Microsoft Office™ computer certificate as well. Maribel decided to quickly add something more to her speech now that the sisters were in the audience.

When Maribel stood up, she opened her remarks by thanking the Waubonsee teachers and students. She paused.

She then thanked Sister Kathleen and Sister Ann for starting her on this journey to learn English, at a time when she soon would have no husband, no money, no papers and no hope. She now realized how much language opened new doors for her with better jobs, more dreams and more friends she was eager to gain … including these two Dominican sisters, who helped to guide her along this path.

Maribel believed they were her guardian angels.

***

Assimilating into a culture also meant enduring what locals experience, including job insecurity. The manufacturing plant where Maribel worked started a crackdown on undocumented immigrants. The shaky work environment now caused Maribel to feel nervous and fearful, wondering what the future would hold for her. She saw workers who were immigrants from different countries, including Africa, India and elsewhere, who suddenly disappeared from their positions in the once-steady workforce.

After nearly a decade at this manufacturer, Maribel now grew nervous with the laws and company policies that involved undocumented immigrants, despite their reputations as reliable and hard workers. She still was not a U.S. citizen. She was not even a permanent resident. It was always something she planned to do, when she found the time, between holding down a job, paying bills and spending time with Mary. She was so thrilled to finally get good health insurance coverage and benefits, that she persevered at her job, landing in the manager's role without looking back. She was making a good wage, paying off her mortgage and saving for the future. She had finally built a reputation as a good worker, someone who was dedicated to helping the company. But she worried now about being revealed as an undocumented immigrant.

She spent several nights thinking about alternative

scenarios. Should she just continue working day by day and hope that no one would find out? If things went sour, and she was let go, would she have enough savings to support her and Mary? Worse, could she be thrown into jail for breaking immigration laws? While questions swirled constantly in her brain, she realized one basic thing: She needed to protect her daughter, no matter what. She had to find a way to move ahead without being caught.

But that decision was about to be made for her.

One day, her boss called her into the office and, without the typical niceties, got right to the point. Was she a legal U.S. resident? If she was, she would have to provide her papers to prove it. The company policy required it and, as her boss, he was obligated to enforce that policy, he told Maribel.

Maribel sat silently for a minute and admitted that she was not a legal U.S. resident. She had nothing to show him, only her work record and company loyalty. Her boss leaned back and sighed.

"Maribel, you have always been a good worker. You easily took on more work and responsibility and we promoted you because you did such a good job. But we have a company policy and we need to uphold it," he said and paused. "Is there any way you have some type of papers, something to show you at least are on track to stay legally in the United States?"

"No. I don't have anything," Maribel said softly.

"I am sorry," he said. "There isn't anything more I can do. I need to let you go, Maribel."

She looked down at her feet, which she had not done since she was at the Dominican Literacy Center. Her admission of her illegal status felt like a strong wind that blew her soul down, trampling her future and everything she worked so hard to accomplish.

"Someday, if you fix this, you could come back," he said.

"I understand," Maribel said. "But first, can you do something for me? Could you provide a letter of recommendation that could help me find another job?"

"I'll be happy to do that," he said.

Maribel was devastated when she lost the manufacturing job. She worked hard, achieved a management position, and learned more about herself in the process. She refused to let this bump in the road stop her now. She was determined to switch gears to find something else that would help to support Mary.

Eventually, she found that new road.

While preparing dinner each night, Maribel would often remember how her mother cooked and how she used to carefully watch the whole process as a young girl, not realizing at the time how she would one day be doing the same thing. Then, whenever Maribel passed a Mexican restaurant, or heard of friends opening a new eatery, she felt she could do a better job. Soon Maribel dreamed of opening her own restaurant. Why not, she thought. She had some savings, and Mary, who was old enough to do some part-time work, started helping with household expenses.

Maribel had a knack for cooking and she remembered her mother's recipes. All she had to do was find a good location.

Maribel then relied on her former brother-in-law for guidance to find a location to open her restaurant. He brought her to some sites that were completely vacant and in busy spots. But Maribel was concerned about investing too much money in building out the space and not having enough money left to invest in the food and workforce.

In 2011, he brought her to a spot in a small strip mall in the south end of Naperville, Illinois. As soon as she walked in, she felt the location was perfect. It felt like hers. It gave her the same feeling as her condo before she bought it. This spot had enough equipment left behind from the previous owner that appeared to be in good, working condition. She then worked with her former brother-in-law and a friend to invest enough to lease the spot and to clean it up.

She named the restaurant Totopos, after the children of some friends voted for the name. It also reminded her of when she was little and her grandmother made corn totopos, a tasty flat, round, or triangular snack, similar to a tortilla, and she left them on the stove to get crispy. She added salt and ate them with her grandmother, who often drank coffee with them. It was a warm memory that Maribel wanted to keep close to her while she worked in the new restaurant.

Totopos opened in the strip mall, which was near a Burger King and a Jewel-Osco grocery store. Inside, she decorated the window sills and a partition with large, fancy bottles of herb-infused olive oil and a few pieces of Mexican art. There were three small tables to seat eight and a side counter with the cash register. The partition separated the eating area from the kitchen, where they would make burritos, tacos, quesadillas, pozole, sopes, gorditas and more. The open design allowed the aromas of the foods to mingle and to entice the customers. Most of all, no one would leave hungry, if she could help it. She did not want anyone to feel the same hunger pangs she once had when cleaning toilets in a department store.

Getting the restaurant ready for its opening day was daunting. But Maribel made sure everything was in place, including a sign with a black background and white lettering that said: "Not fast food. This is authentic Mexican cuisine that is absolutely worth the wait." Maribel placed it near the front door, so it would be the first thing customers would see when they entered.

Among her first customers were Sister Kathleen and Sister Ann, who entered with smiles. They enjoyed seeing their former student parlay her expanding skills into a career as an entrepreneur.

But the blessings from the sisters did not initially help to build a strong clientele for the new restaurant. Few customers came in. Maribel continued to work long hours, but success was elusive. The expenses were outpacing the income and she struggled to make ends meet. Then her partner decided to opt out.

Maribel felt alone as the bills piled up. Tired and aching from another long day, Maribel locked the restaurant's door at night and barely crawled inside her car to drive home. Once the car door closed, she cried.

"I need you, God," Maribel prayed aloud, sitting in the quiet of her car. "I cannot do this alone. I don't have the money to keep this restaurant open."

The next day, when the bills arrived in the mail, Maribel hesitated opening them in fear of the amounts. Still, she sliced open the envelopes. That's when her eyes widened. Luckily, the bills were much lower than expected.

"Amazing," Maribel said aloud. "How can a restaurant operate 10 hours a day and that's all I need to pay for these bills?"

Maribel paid the bills and kept the restaurant operating on a shoestring.

***

In 2013, Maribel started receiving notices in the mail that she was behind in her mortgage payments for the condo and could lose it. All of her savings had been going into the restaurant. She called the bank and asked for a loan modification, but they said she did not qualify. She became more stressed and went home to tell her daughter what she faced.

"You need to pack up your most important things," Maribel told Mary.

"Why, mom?" Mary asked.

"Because we have to leave the house," Maribel said. "I have no money to pay the mortgage anymore and the bank will repossess the house. I have been chasing a stupid and foolish dream with this restaurant and we're losing our house over it."

That night, Maribel could not sleep and began pacing the floor. She then sat down and read the Bible and came across Proverbs 24:27... "Put your outdoor work in order and get your fields ready; after that, build your house." She wondered if God was sending her a message.

That's when Maribel decided to go to the bank and talk to a banker in person about a loan modification. The personal approached worked and the bank officer had Maribel fill out several forms and then sent them along for processing.

Maribel sighed in relief. Her home was saved. She would be able to keep her restaurant open. And her daughter helped to support the household with a new job at a local animal hospital and some babysitting jobs.

Maribel felt God heard her cries. She was determined, more than ever, to make this restaurant work. She continued to go to church on Sundays and prayed to God to help keep Totopos open. She wanted more than to be successful. She wanted her daughter to be proud of her.

Soon some friends from church, Carla and David, who managed a grocery store in Chicago, stopped by the restaurant and brought crates of produce and meats as gifts. While Maribel was surprised by the offer, she quickly turned those packages of tomatoes, avocados, meats and other food into tacos, burritos, quesadillas, tamales and chalupas.

"We know what you must be going through" said Carla. "We used to own a restaurant, too, and know it can be tough at times."

David left a note on the window as he left. It said: "God is on your side."

***

One day a man, looking dirty and disheveled, walked into Totopos, Maribel watched him carefully at first, worried he might steal something. Instead, the man looked at the menu and then slowly turned to leave. Maribel quickly engaged him in conversation to see what his intention was.

"I am hungry, but I don't have any money to buy a meal," the man said.

"Sit down," Maribel told him. She remembered her days of eating day-old bagels out of a trash can and when her cabinets were bare at home.

She then went into the kitchen and returned with a plate packed with food. She placed it before him. The man, wide-eyed, looked at her in wonder.

"Go ahead, eat," Maribel said. "No charge."

The cook, who had just prepared the food, stopped. She never saw Maribel just give away food before, especially when every penny she made was needed for the restaurant.

To Maribel, it was the right thing to do.

***

By 2016, business improved and Totopos was holding its own. Maribel felt secure enough in her savings to start making new plans. After more than 20 years, she wanted to see her mother again. So, she invited her mother to visit her and Mary.

When her mother arrived at O'Hare International Airport in Chicago, it took Maribel a few minutes to recognize her. She remembered how young her mother once looked. Now, she found someone with gray sprinkled through her dark hair, wrinkles on her face and a thinner frame. But Maribel finally recognized her, moved through the crowd and hugged her mother.

Holding each other tight, they began to cry.

Maribel eagerly chauffeured her mother around in her new car to show her the highlights of Chicago and the suburbs. But the biggest highlight was showing her where she first learned English. Maribel took her mother to meet Sister Kathleen at the literacy center. The two older women, who each taught Maribel different lessons in life, hugged each other as if they were old friends.

Learning English was such a turning point for Maribel and she felt a strong need to introduce Sister Kathleen to her mother. They had played a big role in her transformation and helped her learn how to dream. When Maribel was married, she was not allowed to dream between the beatings. But Sister Ann and Sister Kathleen opened her eyes in such a peaceful way.

Sure, it was difficult and, at times, frustrating to learn English. But Maribel chose to dream. It led to better jobs, a savings account, an education for her daughter, her first car, her first home and now her first restaurant. Can you imagine choosing to dream? That was something new for Maribel. But, fortunately, many of these dreams became a reality.

***

Long after her mother returned to Mexico, Maribel drove a friend to the Mexican Consulate to get an ID. While she waited in the lobby for her friend, Maribel looked at some of the posters on the walls and was drawn to one that promoted the U Visa, which could lead to U.S. residency.

The U Visa intrigued her. If she was a victim of a crime, she could qualify. She would need to obtain a police report and talk to a lawyer at the consulate. She felt that she qualified and could apply for it. Why not? It was time.

She briefly talked to a lawyer at the consulate, who explained the steps she needed to take to qualify for the U Visa. He gave her phone numbers of six agencies to call for assistance.

After she returned home, Maribel called five of the agencies and hit dead ends. Finally, the sixth number, World Relief, said it could help her. She made an appointment.

When Maribel arrived at World Relief, she talked about her interest in getting a U Visa. They said she qualified as a victim of domestic violence because of the beatings she endured from her husband, how she finally called the police and reported her husband, and how she followed through with an order of protection and a divorce. She needed a copy of that police report and her divorce papers. She gathered them in the next few days and returned.

That's when they told her she needed one more thing: a letter from the lawyer who handled her divorce.

After about 20 years, she wondered if her former attorney, Patrick Kinnally, would remember her. He probably handled hundreds of divorce cases since she left her husband and wondered if he was even in the same office. She then tracked down Kinnally and learned he was, indeed, still in Aurora.

Now, Maribel wondered if he would even be willing to see her. After all, she had spent the last 20 years in the United States as an illegal alien. Some would say she had plenty of opportunities to correct her situation. How would he be able to handle this? She called his office and made an appointment for the following month, his earliest time available.

When she arrived at Kinnally's office, she had her divorce papers in hand, just in case he needed to refresh his memory. As it turned out, that wasn't necessary. He asked her how she and her daughter were doing.

Maribel was surprised he remembered. Perhaps he had reviewed her file, she thought.

"Mary is still living with me and helping me," Maribel said. She then filled him in on her restaurant.

"You did a good job," he said, nodding. "Back when you wanted the divorce, I asked you how you would survive, because you refused support, and you said you would work really hard. Now, you're a restaurant owner. I'm proud of you. But what brings you in now?"

Maribel paused. She never had anyone say they were proud of her before. She absorbed that moment quickly.

"I need a letter from you," Maribel said. "I applied for a U Visa and provided the documents they needed. Now, I just need a letter from you since you handled my divorce."

"I am not going to do that," Patrick said.

Maribel's heart dropped and she was surprised that he refused so quickly.

"Instead, I am going to represent you, so you can become a legal permanent resident," Kinnally said. "And, I am not going to charge you for my services. But because you have been an illegal alien, you will need to pay a penalty to the immigration authorities."

Maribel agreed. Luckily, she had enough savings to cover the penalty. She then immediately started the process to become a permanent resident. He told her she would have to wait about four years before she could apply to become a U.S. citizen.

"You know, when I first met you, I was afraid of you," Maribel said. "But I am not afraid anymore."

**

Every year, Maribel wanted to try something new, whether it was a new food or a place she has never visited. Then one day at the Calvary Church service in Naperville, another new challenge opened: a marathon.

It was a particularly hard week at the restaurant, trying to keep up with a growing customer base and then cleaning and preparing the kitchen for each day. The stress was taking a toll on her health. She was tired and even gained a few pounds on her short frame. So, when the international Christian humanitarian organization, World Vision, came to her church to make a presentation in 2017, she perked up. They were recruiting runners for the Chicago Marathon. If they could form a church team, they could raise money to help the poor. Those who were already runners could fulfill a lifelong dream of running in the Chicago Marathon and others could welcome the opportunity of helping others.

Maribel toyed with the idea of becoming a marathon runner. But she never ran in her life, let alone such an iconic race with thousands of others who were far more experienced. She couldn't even run from the restaurant to her car in the parking lot during a rainstorm. Physically, she was untrained and out of shape. Her routine consisted of working long hours at the restaurant, taking care of the necessities at home and trying to get some sleep.

But there was something attractive about outrunning the wind, running free without any bonds, leaving behind the world and speeding into the future. It also would feel good to help someone in need by raising money through the race, Maribel thought.

The challenge of running 26 miles piqued her interest, but apparently not Mary's. When Maribel brought up the idea to Mary, her daughter resisted.

"You cannot do it," Mary said. "You don't have the time. And you could get sick just trying to do it."

Maribel suddenly felt the need surge inside of her, urging her to accomplish this new challenge. Now, whenever she was told she could not do something, she wanted to prove them wrong. She no longer was held back by an ex-husband, who consistently told her she was worthless, who said she would never amount to anything and that she could not do anything right. All the things her ex-husband said and repeated, just reverberated in her mind: "You are stupid. You cannot do anything good."

No. Not this time, Maribel thought.

"I have to do this. I am not the person you said I am," Maribel said to herself, as if telling off her ex-husband's memory.

Maribel contacted World Vision, got the instructions to train for the marathon and joined the team from her church. Many were already runners and they gladly offered advice and guidance to her.

While Maribel worried if she could properly train and even run the race, she thought of the consequences of her decision. What if she entered, started the training and then decided it was just too tough to continue? Would that mean she would be a quitter? Was her ex-husband right? What would that show her daughter? Would Mary think it would be OK to start and then stop something, just because it was too difficult?

Maribel was not going to be a quitter. She needed to move ahead, regardless of how tough it would be. She wanted to teach her daughter that you do not quit just because something is hard to accomplish. She felt a need to teach her daughter to finish whatever is in front of her. Maribel also remembered her mother and her 16-hour days of selling produce at a market in Mexico to feed her family. Her mother kept going. Maribel would, too.

"What are you going to accomplish?" said Mary. "It will be very hard for you."

"I just want to do this," Maribel insisted.

Her accomplishment would be discipline and endurance, a promise made and a promise kept.

Maribel read the training papers. They said, in part, to run one minute, walk two minutes. Gradually work up to running five minutes, then walk a couple of minutes. Just keep building on that momentum.

The weather was still bone-chilling cold and damp on that day in March 2017. Maribel pushed herself to get outside that first day and every day that followed, keeping the instructions in mind and what she could do. She even partnered with others from church during those training sessions and closely watched the regular runners. She learned how to pace herself, how to stand, how to stretch, how to move her feet and legs, and how and when to eat and drink while running longer distances in order to keep up her strength.

Participants from church broke into smaller groups according to their speed. Maribel desperately did not want to be part of the last group with the slowest runners. So, she kept challenging herself to do a little extra every day. If the instructions said to run one mile, Maribel would run two miles.

Mary watched her mother struggle but also saw how much she was improving. Soon, Maribel could run one mile. Then two miles. Then three miles.

By May 2017, Maribel was ready to tackle her first 5K race, or 3.1 miles. She was already exhausted from the training and wondered if she could even finish. The World Vision teams were lined up and Maribel heard the starting gun.

She was finally pacing in her first race, as if her life depended on it. She thought of her ex-husband and the blows that drew blood, broke her nose and tore her skin. That hurt turned into anger and then fury. She then turned that all into more energy. She gritted her teeth and felt, instead of the sting of her ex-husband's blows, the cooling trickle of sweat from a job she trained for with purpose and direction.

She finished the 5K. She was so amazed, she almost forgot how sore her entire body felt. She also earned her first paper medal from the group. Although it was just paper, it was a strong symbol. It was an incentive that spoke to her, softly saying that she can run a real marathon. She can do this. She knew then she would continue.

Soon, Maribel was running nine miles throughout the area, Monday through Friday. She gradually increased her mileage by pushing herself a little extra each day. She started running by herself — feeling the wind streak across her face, passing the green trees and bushes and parked cars — and loving her new sense of freedom. It also became a time between herself and God. While she ran, she prayed. Her mind raced with her body. She also stopped complaining of any muscle aches. She felt the training sessions were becoming more like blessings.

She also brought her training experiences to work at Totopos, talking briefly each day with customers who jogged in. She shared her marathon training experiences with them. Soon, customers were delighted to hear of her daily stories, and how her mileage and stamina increased. Maribel loved hearing their encouragement. It gave her a new sense of excitement, because she was becoming a part of something bigger than herself.

One older woman, who was also a runner, encouraged Maribel to keep training for the marathon, even if it felt like she would never make it.

"Just run," the woman said.

But sometimes, Maribel felt like this marathon was a crazy dream and not for her, and even considered quitting. She was too busy at the restaurant to keep pushing off her responsibilities onto another worker. Even Mary was starting to cook breakfast for her daily — oatmeal and fruit with almond milk.

Mary also began buying new, trendier clothing or socks designed just for runners and gifting them to her mother. Then, Maribel and Mary went to a store to get her feet measured so she could buy proper running shoes. While Maribel picked out a brand-name pair that was highly recommended, she cringed at the $150 price tag. Luckily, a clerk pointed her to the clearance rack where a similar pair in her size cost just $40. The savings thrilled Maribel and she immediately felt the difference in running after she laced them up for the first time.

Besides the cost of the shoes, the ongoing costs of participating in the marathon worried Maribel. She was spending a lot of money each day on her training and on hiring extra workers to maintain Totopos in her absence. Was it worth it? She wondered. But her customers at the restaurant said it was. So, she kept going.

The constant training also made her feel like she was doing something good. It would help raise money for those in poverty, an experience that Maribel will never forget, especially those stale bagels from the garbage can.

In addition, Maribel loved getting daily notes from Mary, who saw the changes in her mother and only wanted to give her hope, encouragement and a deeper sense of love.

"It doesn't matter the time, it's the finish. You are my winner." Such notes from Mary kept Maribel motivated.

By the time she was about to reach the next milestone of 20 miles, Maribel hesitated. It actually made her think twice. It even intimidated her.

"God, why are you putting me here? Maybe I should pray for a huge storm to stop the marathon?" Maribel thought.

She shook it off and continued. After everything she had been through in life, Maribel knew now she was not a quitter.

Maribel thought she might accomplish those 20 miles if she ran with someone in her church group on the World Vision team. So, she texted Danny, a friend from church who was experienced in races, and asked him to run with her. They decided to meet at a park in Naperville. He was better and faster than Maribel and it could encourage her to reach that 20-mile goal.

On one Saturday morning around 5:30, Maribel and Danny paused to say a prayer and then took off. They easily ran nine miles, but they ran out of water. They stopped at a nearby bathroom and refilled their bottles. By this time, Danny was hurting and was starting to have difficulty moving ahead. As they continued, Danny started falling behind as they approached their 17-mile mark. He finally came to a stop.

"I'm done," Danny said, breathless. "I cannot do anymore. The pain in my leg is too much."

Maribel worried about his pain. She then wondered how it would affect their running partnership and how much she depended on his encouragement.

Danny needed to sit out of the rest of their training. Yet, Maribel was determined to finish. While Danny rested, Maribel continued alone. Alone. The word itself chilled her. Yet, surprisingly, it soon felt amazing. While she was alone, she somehow realized she could do this. She could finish 20 miles on her own.

As she reached her 20-mile limit for the first time, her body heaved for air and her limbs shook, yet she experienced an invigorating sense of accomplishment rushing through her soul. That's when she knew, at that moment, that she could tackle 26 miles. That meant she could run the whole marathon.

When she later met with others in her group from Calvary, World Vision showed a video on other races and what it was like to finish. While some breezed through, many other runners collapsed or hobbled over the finish line, gasping for air, sweating profusely, all while someone tossed a blanket over them.

As Maribel watched, she slowly became nervous. She was

worried about being in physical pain and thought she wasn't ready to tackle the marathon. Her feelings bounced back and forth. Ready. Not ready. Ready. Her nerves were like electrical wires.

***

By September 2017, one month before the Chicago Marathon, Maribel's leg was hurting and she made an appointment with a doctor. After an exam, the doctor told Maribel that one leg was actually shorter than the other and the running had thrown her spine off balance. The speed and the repetitive pattern of running would become detrimental, if she continued. He recommended that she stop running.

"I cannot stop. Not now. I am so close," Maribel said, determined to finish this crazy dream. "What's the worst that could happen?"

The doctor outlined the damage she could face, including a hip replacement in the future. She paused. A hip replacement? God, she did not want to damage her body. But she must finish what she started. She decided to stay on track for the marathon.

To address her pain, in the meantime, the doctor insisted that she go to physical therapy three times a week. It would get her through this race.

She followed his orders, yet the physical therapy itself often was painful. But she reassured herself, it would only last a short while. Her goal was just to get through this crazy bucket-list goal.

Just one more month.

Maribel also learned many people at church and at her restaurant were cheering for her and praying that she would finish the marathon safely. Customers would plunk down their credit cards or a few dollars for food, then tell her to keep going, work hard and she would finish the marathon. Those words were the fuel she needed.

*****

Maribel and her team from Calvary wore their World Vision orange, white and blue diagonally striped T-shirts and dark spandex shorts when they arrived in downtown Chicago about 4:30 a.m. on the day of the Chicago Marathon. It was dark and cold that early October morning as thousands of others were arriving before the 8 a.m. shotgun start.

By 7 a.m., officials began moving her and her team to a starting corral as they watched long lines of racers wind around the outlying portable toilets.

Finally, all the runners were lined up. Some did last-minute stretches for their calves, while others breathed in deeply and shook their arms and legs to reinvigorate themselves in the cold air.

Then, as the moment arrived, the gun blasted, and the

runners took off. Bodies flowed along, keeping pace, in a wave of colors. Maribel finally was a part of her first marathon, and she watched as the spectators blended together along the fenced-off sidelines. She suddenly heard someone calling her name. Some of her friends saw her and waved wildly, as if to send their energy and bolstered her with a surge of strength. Then strangers started hooting and yelling as she passed. The energy thrilled and invigorated her, so much so, that she left behind her fears from all those months of training and enjoyed the moment.

Maribel quickly turned around and spotted a sea of runners, all coming up in waves behind her. She was enveloped in the river of bodies flowing this way and that, weaving through Chicago's neighborhoods from the north side to the south side. She avoided landing on sewer covers and deep cracks in the pavement and kept tabs on her running buddies from church because some were starting to lag.

By the 15-mile marker, one of her teammates got hurt. Maribel and a few others quickly tried to get her up and running again. But she stayed behind, while Maribel and the team continued.

By the time Maribel reached Chinatown, she had achieved 20 miles. But her stomach began to hurt and she didn't drink much water. So, she grabbed a paper cup and then a banana along the way. Someone then handed her a cookie and it seemed so deliciously sweet on her tongue, like a well-earned prize. She kept going, almost as if she was on autopilot.

Maribel looked in the distance and saw the John Hancock building and realized just how far she had come. By this time, her sports bra was chafing and her shoes were scratching her toes. Her body screamed at her to stop. But she pushed ahead. She refused to quit now.

She watched as she passed the marathon markers. Only three more miles to go. She thought it was comparable to the distance from the park to her house and tried to visualize how easy that was to do. But those last few miles seemed like the longest and roughest in her life.

After that, she didn't remember counting the rest of the mile markers as she alternated her pace from running then walking and then running again. Then she heard Mary's voice. It was like entering the gates of Heaven. Her eyes widened as she frantically searched for her whereabouts and heard a familiar voice.

"Run! Run!" Mary bellowed at her mother. "LET'S GOOOOO!!!"

Maribel mustered whatever energy she had left. She willed herself to not quit, especially in front of her wonderful, beautiful, college-educated daughter. Maribel had to prove to Mary that her mother was not a quitter.

She. Had. To. Finish.

The finish line was so close, and Maribel's heart was leaping out of her chest. She had another bridge and a hill ahead of her and, again, she felt like she would not make it. But she also knew she was not far from realizing her goal, the grand finale of training so hard for so long.

Just then, another team member reached out for Maribel and, like a natural reflex, Maribel slowed for what seemed like nanoseconds to grasp her colleague's hand to ensure they were connected. The last bits of energy they each had mingled as their eyes met. Without words, they just knew they could do this. And they finally went through the finish line together.

The public address system announced Maribel's name and time: 6 hours, 33 minutes. She missed automatically qualifying for next year's marathon by a mere 3 seconds, which felt like a lifetime.

She then heard the clapping and saw more spectators. The thrill of finishing ran through her, along with a shakiness of her body attempting to shift back into normal gear and her soul still soaring to Heaven.

Maribel was amazed. Grateful. Humbled.

In only seven months, Maribel accomplished what many runners do after years of training. She ran and finished her first marathon, driven by her determination to finish her goal, to help raise money for charity and to challenge herself to do good. Throughout her mission, her soul was fed by her fellow participants from church and her customers, all while her heart was fed by her wonderful, supportive daughter. Mary ensured that her body was properly fed for this new battle and her heart was filled with love.

Maribel also left behind a world of hurt, anger and despair, proving in the shadow of her ex-husband's abuse that she, indeed, could do something good and worthwhile. Her sweat and pain turned into an accomplishment that she never thought was possible.

She outran the wind. She was free. She finished a marathon, in more ways than one. She then paused to say a prayer.

"Why did you wait for your friend? You could have finished more quickly on your own and qualified," Mary asked, jogging up to her mother and then hugging her.

"I wasn't going to leave her behind," Maribel said. "We finished together. That's what really counts."

Mary paused and knew what her mother meant and she loved her even more. Maribel smiled and just kept breathing deeply and trying to make her body wind down as she continued to take small steps to cool her raging skin.

After Maribel cooled down and gathered with her family

on the street, she asked where they would go out to celebrate. Instead, Mary insisted that her mother go home and rest.

"But I'm not tired," Maribel insisted. The adrenaline was hard to curb and it continued to race through her as if she was still on the course. Maribel was too pumped to just go home and take a nap. But she relented and they returned home.

Instead of going to bed, Maribel immediately went outside on her bicycle and soon cycled about three miles. The weather turned warm and sunny. Her eyes opened wide and she drank in the day and a goal that was unthinkable just a few years ago. Despite her fears and nervousness, she felt a sense of true accomplishment. Between her successes with earning a living, getting a car and a driver's license, saving for a home, opening her own restaurant and, now, finishing a marathon, Maribel was no longer "stupid." She was no longer "worthless."

She thanked God for the beautiful day. She thanked God that she had finished the marathon.

Finally, she thanked God for the many blessings and gifts in her life: the gift of English that opened many doors to new and better jobs, her many friendships and her own restaurant. Those gifts helped to push her to finish the marathon. Looking back at her pain and anguish over her divorce, it all led to these gifts in disguise because it gave her a chance to rediscover herself, her self-esteem and her self-worth. She learned to love and respect herself. She gained wisdom and confidence through every setback and accomplishment.

She wouldn't let anyone put her down anymore, not for any reason. God changed her life and let her learn what she needed to do in order to survive and to accomplish things she never dreamt were possible. In fact, she finally was capable of having dreams and then she set goals and achieved them. It gave her a sense of finally fitting into a good life.

Maribel felt like she had come through a long, dark tunnel and emerged into the light. She was no longer reliving those episodes where her ex-husband nearly beat the life out of her and her dreams. She had her own life now. While she thought she could erase many of those bad memories from her mind, they refused to leave. In the past, she surrendered herself as a human being and as a woman to brutality so cruel that the life was kicked out of her. Those memories hurt. But now, she was just a spectator to those bad memories.

The rest of her was finally free.

Maribel smiled, a giant, cheek-breaking smile as tears of joy rolled down her cheeks.

***

A few weeks after the marathon, Maribel sent $1,000 to her sister, Virginia, in Mexico to buy shoes and jackets for anyone she found on the streets who needed help. Maribel wanted to give something back to the people of her homeland, especially those who were barely getting by, just like she experienced after her divorce. It was her way of saying thank you to God. Her restaurant was doing better. Her life with her daughter was on track and Mary had a nice boyfriend.

Maribel was able to cross things off her bucket list, like completing the marathon and preparing for U.S. citizenship.

Next, she wanted to return something to her former homeland in Tlaxcala, Mexico. She originally left Mexico about 24 years ago to reunite with her abusive husband and, instead, left behind her self-respect and self-confidence. Now, her heart was full, and she had so much more, including her self-esteem, her self-confidence, the completion of a marathon and a few extra dollars she earned herself from her own business.

"Virginia, I don't know your neighbors, so ask around," Maribel said to her sister on the phone. "Who needs some help? Some new shoes? A sweater? Or a jacket? I'll send the money and you can buy those things for them."

Virginia agreed. She lived in Puebla, Mexico, and had two children. She also was a grandmother and felt the sting of seeing one too many children in the area go without shoes or a jacket. She didn't have far to go to find people in need. There often were adults, hunched over, fending off the wind just outside her door. Or children washing car windows to earn a few pesos. Or an elderly woman in the market selling a few trinkets, but who still could not afford a new pair of shoes for herself.

Whenever Virginia went to work in the morning at her shop, she would peruse the streets outside. Maribel's $1,000 would have at least double the value there and could buy plenty of shoes and coats. Whenever she came across someone who walked by the shop frequently, she stopped and talked with them. She found out their age, where they were going and how long they went without something warm.

When they passed the store again, Virginia left behind a customer, quickly grabbed a parcel and ran out the door to catch the child or elderly person to give them a sweater or some shoes. Their initial shock turned to a huge smile as Virginia helped them put on the item. She also snapped a quick photo with the new item each time and sent it to Maribel. Mission accomplished, Virginia said.

As the holidays approached, Maribel decided to visit Tlaxcala. She went to her sister's shop and they partnered again, this time with goody bags filled with pencils, small candies and other items.

They stood in the middle of the marketplace and started handing out dozens of small goody bags. The children looked up in surprise and snatched the bags before the gifts could disappear. They quickly looked inside, then looked up at Maribel or Virginia and scurried away to enjoy their treats.

Maribel smiled, which came naturally and freely now. It was a joy to see the looks of surprise and happiness as the children accepted her gifts. It also gave her joy to see her homeland smile back instead of being a place of pain and lost dreams.

***

In early 2019, Maribel was excited that Mary was serious about her boyfriend and began wondering if the two would marry. Mary was 29 years old and at a good stage in her life. She first met her boyfriend while attending Northern Illinois University. But Mary was serious about school and wanted to finish before landing a job at a local animal hospital. Mary saw him again during a reunion and they ran into each other one other time, which led to their relationship.

Maribel was concerned and immediately felt protective of her little girl. Yes, Mary was now a grown woman. But Maribel was concerned about her boyfriend's motives. Would he treat her daughter with love and respect? Would he be a good provider and protect her from hunger? All Maribel could do was pray that he would be a good choice.

When Mary was 15, she did not have a quinceañera because she didn't want her mother to spend so much money on a beautiful gown and all the trimmings to introduce her to society. Mary knew Maribel didn't have the money at the time.

Yet, Maribel would have been more than willing to sacrifice for her daughter so she could mark her passage from girlhood to womanhood.

Besides, Maribel always heard her daughter say she would never marry, especially after seeing what happened to her mother for so many years. Maribel felt sad, knowing that her daughter may have heard more than she should have when her husband started beating her behind closed doors.

So, when Mary told Maribel that she was serious about her boyfriend and they discussed marriage, Maribel was excited yet cautious. She wanted Mary to be happy, but safe. She wanted Mary to love and to be loved. After her boyfriend proposed, Mary had a look of pure joy in her eyes. Maribel could not deny her daughter anything and, in fact, she was ready to splurge on a wedding.

But just like a quinceañera, Mary said she was not interested in a big wedding reception. It would be too expensive and too stressful to plan. Mary just wanted to get married in a very simple way. In fact, she told Maribel that when she and her fiancé get married, they would just go to a judge at the local courthouse and have a civil ceremony. It would be quick and inexpensive.

One night, Mary talked with her mother about another matter. Mary had one more thing to do.

She wanted to see a lawyer about her own citizenship status. Since she arrived in the United States as a little girl at a time when Maribel was seeking a better life, Mary was still considered a Dreamer, a citizen of Mexico. So, Mary did what her mother did. She went to a lawyer to apply for permanent residency and get on track to attain U.S. citizenship. The Dreamer was realizing her own dream to become a U.S. citizen and to have a future with someone she loved and would be with for a long time.

Maribel understood her daughter and loved her even more for it. Mary was her own woman, just like her mom.

***

As March approached, Mary's fiancé had an aunt who was battling cancer and starting to fade. He had hoped to get married before she died. And Maribel's mother, who was visiting, was planning to return soon to Mexico. So, the young couple told their parents they planned to get married soon at the courthouse, so the aunt and grandmother could be a part of it. Mary asked Maribel to keep it a secret from her grandmother, because they wanted to surprise her.

As the days passed, Maribel rushed around to buy nice outfits for herself and her mother for the wedding day. She kept insisting her mother look nice for the wedding of Mary's "friend." Maribel also bought flowers and made the bridal bouquet, corsages and boutonnieres for family members.

On the day of the wedding, Maribel fussed over her daughter, so she would look just right, and handed out flowers to everyone. Maribel's mother wondered why everyone was so nervous just attending the wedding of a "friend." Then she saw Mary's fiancé dressed nicely in a dark suit and said, "I want you to marry my granddaughter."

"Really?" the groom said, acting surprised. After some good-natured teasing, he stopped and smiled. "Yes, I am marrying your granddaughter today."

The grandmother smiled and Maribel started to tear up. Maribel had been praying for a good husband for her daughter. She asked God to send a good man, who would take care of her. She was assured that this was the right man.

During the civil ceremony, Maribel watched Mary, who was elegantly dressed in a peach-colored dress. They exchanged their vows and their rings. Tears then began to spill down Maribel's cheeks. Years ago, it would have been hard to even imagine this day. Now, Maribel was imagining the future without pain and without anguish. The love from this day was deeply felt by Maribel, and she reveled in such a blessing.

While the ceremony was quick and simple, it was powerful. It now meant her daughter was one with this man and Maribel approved. She still could not believe her little girl had grown up and was now married. Maribel recalled some of the horrors of her own marriage and shuddered.

Thankfully, she now saw Mary glow with happiness. That's what counted.

Chapter 20

JUANITA INCREASES HER CONFIDENCE

By 1997, Juanita earned a certificate from the Dominican Literacy Center. While she was bursting with pride, she also regretted leaving behind both her lessons and Sister Kathleen. Besides learning English, she also learned about life, about raising her family and about herself. She felt like she was emerging from a cocoon and was wondering what would come next.

Juanita was ready for that next step: taking classes to become a U.S. citizen.

Jaime had already become a citizen and he was now encouraging his wife to do the same. She had come a long way from being insecure to becoming a more secure, yet humble woman, who handled the children and household with ease and independence.

Juanita studied hard in the classes to learn about her

adopted homeland and, eventually, was prepared to take the test to become a U.S. citizen. She traveled with Jaime to downtown Chicago and walked into the federal building, filled out the paperwork and waited for her name to be called.

When her name was announced, she walked into a room where a man tested her knowledge of the United States. She was alone with the tester, and she could not look for Jaime or any other familiar face for support. She was completely on her own. But this time, she drew upon her new-found confidence and her lessons. She had studied and she knew the answers. After about an hour, she was told that she had passed.

***

Later, Juanita participated in the oath ceremony and held a small American flag for the first time. She stood toward the front of the group of dozens of other people from around the world. They also were holding a small American flag, all coveting their new dreams in their adopted country.

The judge asked everyone to raise their right hands to take the oath. As they continued to hold the flags in their left hands, they recited the oath of U.S. citizenship.

Juanita said the words in English. It felt normal. Emotional. Happy. She now closed one door and opened another. Just like that.

"Now, I can vote," she thought. "I can do a lot of things. I have a voice."

It was an inner voice that was growing stronger for some time. She was a wife and mother and now she was a new U.S. citizen. She was a part of something bigger than herself. It was scary, yet exciting. It emboldened her.

"I did this for me, first," she told Jaime. "And then I did it for you and the kids."

Afterward, Juanita and Jaime went to eat at a restaurant in downtown Chicago to celebrate. During dinner, she suddenly stopped and put down her fork. The impact of becoming a U.S. citizen was finally settling in. Juanita began to feel a bit sad. She knew she had left behind poverty and ignorance and fear. Still, she was born and raised in Mexico and it was her homeland.

"Am I betraying Mexico?" she asked Jaime.

"No," he said. "You are making them proud."

"I feel good, even happy. It is a sense of accomplishment," Juanita told Jaime. "It felt good to be a part of a big group when I was taking the oath. But when you are tested, it's just you alone. Then I received an American flag. They put it in my hand. And you were with me. I felt comfortable. I felt free and strong. But, also, I felt more power to help others as well."

Chapter 21

BLANCA ENJOYS A 20-YEAR CAREER

In 1997, Blanca received her much-anticipated promotion to supervisor along with a raise at the medical center. She was thrilled to rise above the ranks of being a housekeeper. As a supervisor now, she managed a diverse group of 25 housekeepers. Blanca never anticipated advancing in any job, let alone one in the United States. But it happened. And she felt she owed much of it to the English language lessons at the Dominican Literacy Center. That helped to open doors and gave her opportunities she may not have gotten otherwise. The extra income that came with the promotion also helped her family. It boosted their savings, which allowed them to buy a nicer home in the Fox Valley region. The new neighborhood and school district also provided better educational opportunities for her children, so they could flourish.

She also continued to learn how to manage people,

document their work and mentor a team. Luckily, the promotion also provided more management training and computer classes. Those, too, opened additional doors to meet and work with more people, who believed in her and her skills. They wanted to see her succeed.

While Blanca was excited about her promotion and new opportunities, it also meant spending more time away from her husband and children. Evenings and weekends were spent working. But she knew the sacrifices she needed to make for her family to survive and to thrive financially.

***

Those years of enjoying her job were reaching a different type of milestone that Blanca never expected. In 2010, she arrived at her office to start her workday, which was expected to be just like any other day. But this time, she was blindsided by an announcement of a mass layoff. After a flurry of closed-door meetings, Blanca's heart was heavy, and she took the news personally. It appeared to be the end of a successful path she had loved for the last 21 years.

The losses of jobs, prestige and wages were not her fault or the fault of her colleagues and subordinates. A combination of factors contributed to situations like this, especially when the Great Recession already chipped away at many companies. She was told that the executives decided to outsource its janitorial services to save money so it could remain viable in the medical field.

Still, it upset Blanca. Not only was she losing a job that she loved, but she was being forced to say farewell to her colleagues, and many of them had shared their hopes and aspirations and everyday lives with her. Instead of sharing those dreams with each other today, they now were sharing looks of uncertainty of the future, concerns about paying their rent or mortgages and other bills. Many of them had fears about putting enough food on the table for their families.

Also, Blanca faced another level of concern beyond her younger colleagues. She needed to think about what to do before she signed the separation papers. She was 61 years old. Would it be harder to get another job now at an older age and with her physical limitations? For years, she had suffered from debilitating migraines multiple times a week, back pain that led to many surgeries and crippling fibromyalgia that permeated her body. Then, there was osteoarthritis, most likely from years of wear and tear from stretching, kneeling and bending as a housekeeper. The daily pain she experienced was a cross that she carried for decades.

Those health matters led to countless days when she wished she could just stay in bed, lay down for long periods of time or call in sick to her job. But she did not do that. She had all the responsibilities of a full-time job along with parenting three children, managing a home and its budget. Only through prayer and seeking God's mercy and compassion on those days did she find the strength and perseverance to endure.

After the layoff announcement, Blanca talked with her family. They helped her to realize this push into retirement could be good. After all, Eusebio already was retired after working for about 45 years. She could now join him and enjoy the future with him. She had a successful ride with a U.S. company and that made her happy. It helped her and Eusebio to save money, to raise their children and to walk two of them down the aisle in marriage. They even welcomed the birth of their first grandchild, Sebastian. They also were able to afford a comfortable home in North Aurora and to take return trips to Mexico to visit family.

Blanca decided to sign the separation papers and then she officially retired at age 62.

"I'm done," Blanca told Eusebio. "God gave me a lot of blessings."

***

Blanca realized later that the computer training she received while at the medical center helped her to appreciate other new technology. She later learned to use an iPhone and an iPad. She also delved into the Internet and social media. In fact, she loved quickly sharing photos with friends and family and exploring the web. She also learned how to use Facetime, so she could be instantly connected to her family and friends around Mexico.

It also allowed her to see how things were going in her hometown of Marin, Mexico, all while living in North Aurora. To be transported thousands of miles in just seconds was miraculous and she thanked God every day that she could learn new things to keep in touch with her loved ones.

She never felt too old for any of this. Those connections made her happy. It made her feel closer to them, as if they were always with her.

Chapter 22

TERESA'S STRENGTH FUELS HER GOALS

By 1998, Teresa was thrilled when she earned a certificate from the Dominican Literacy Center and felt confident enough to use English wherever she went. It was time now to achieve her other goals. Teresa then applied for permanent residency and got a green card in 2001. She also learned how to drive and received her driver's license.

Then, she and her husband left behind their life in a mobile home and saved enough to buy a single-family home, where they could raise their children.

But one day, Teresa opened a door inside their home and looked in terror as black smoke from a fire had quickly enveloped her. Luckily, no one else was home at the time. She then ran to a neighbor's house for help and they called the fire department.

When word about the fire reached the center, Sister Ann

and some tutors arrived to offer consolation to Teresa and her family and gave them some donated blankets and food.

***

As the years passed and her children grew up, Teresa returned to work, this time at a factory on Route 31, where she produced paint sample cards. She worked at the factory for about 1 ½ years before switching to a job at an electronics factory.

By this time, Teresa longed to become a U.S. citizen and fulfill another of her long-held dreams. She already had watched as Miguel studied and then became a U.S. citizen in 2000.

By 2005, she started taking the citizenship classes, studied hard and prepared to take the test. She fit the course load in between her factory shifts and raising her children. She felt the stress was worth it.

When the day came, Teresa was nervous, sitting alone with a tester from Immigration. It intimidated her. But she answered the questions and was thrilled later when she learned that she had passed the test and could participate in the oath ceremony.

On the day she was scheduled to take the oath to become a U.S. citizen, Teresa worked an all-night shift, went home, took a shower and then took a taxi to the train station. She then jumped on the commuter train to downtown Chicago. She was excited and tired, no doubt, after having no sleep. But this was one of the most important days of her life.

When she arrived at the downtown Chicago courthouse, she stood in a room with dozens of other people, holding a small flag and repeating, in English, the oath to become a U.S. citizen.

Chapter 23

MARIA LANDS CITIZENSHIP AND A JOB

In 2000, Maria earned her certificate of completion from the Dominican Literacy Center and sought Sister Ann's help to earn her GED. After she achieved the GED, Maria wanted to become a U.S. citizen and took more classes at the center to prepare for the U.S. citizenship test.

Acting like the tester, Sister Ann quizzed Maria to make sure she didn't get too nervous if an unexpected question was tossed at her. And since Valentin had already taken the test to become a citizen a few years earlier, Maria borrowed his book on citizenship preparation and studied it in earnest.

By 2002, Maria was worried that she would become confused while taking the oral exam for U.S. citizenship. Her tester asked her a question and Maria smiled. He smiled, too.

She then repeated his question, just so she could get it right. She did. At the end, he said she passed and relief swept over her.

"Do you want to change your name?" the tester asked.

"My name at birth was Maria de Jesus Chavez Torres," Maria said. "But after becoming a resident and getting my driver's license, I'll use my married name of Maria Dominguez."

Maria walked out and started to cry. Valentin walked up to her and was unsure of what may have happened with the tester. Did she pass or not? Were those tears of joy or discouragement? Wide-eyed, he stood in front of her, waiting anxiously for the outcome.

"I made it!" Maria declared with a smile.

"See, I told you that you could do it!" said a relieved Valentin, a smile spreading across his face.

Later, Maria participated in the oath ceremony with a group of people from around the world. She raised her right hand and, deep inside, she felt proud of herself and how far she finally came to reach this day.

After taking the U.S. citizenship oath, Maria somehow felt safer — as if the past was gone with all its fear and anxiety — and her future was clearer, brighter and more secure. It was a dream that had come true, a miracle that she hadn't expected. Valentin said the sisters at the Dominican Literacy Center had helped her to get this far.

"You found your angels," he said.

"I've been improving myself and it was something I wanted to do for myself, not just for my family," Maria told him. "I always thought I was not intelligent, or it was hard for me to learn or to retain information. But this worked and I am so happy with the United States."

Maria's heart swelled. She never thought that when she came from Mexico that she could do this. The Dominican sisters were a big influence on her life. If she had to choose again between Mexico and the United States, she told Valentin, she would choose the United States. She was happy here. She no longer had any regrets about her decision to stay.

Now that both her English program and the citizenship classes were finished, Maria just didn't want to leave the center. She felt safe there. Somehow, she felt like she was losing her family at the center. It was also a time when Maria learned to trust Americans and she felt that they would not be mean to her or to her children. She felt more secure and confident now that she knew English and could fit in better with her new society. She was finally feeling that she was at home in the United States.

***

One day in 2005, Maria received a call from Sister Kathleen because the center needed additional office help and they had the funds to hire someone. She offered Maria a part-time job, two days a week and possibly five hours each day.

But the thought of working at the center made Maria nervous. She would need to always answer the calls in English and understand the callers as they spoke English to her. Would she be able to help them?

"I don't know if I can do it," Maria said. "You can find someone with a college degree, and they would understand English better."

Sister Kathleen persisted. "We know," Sister Kathleen said. "But we want you. We will teach you what you need to know, and we will help you along the way."

Tears welled up in Maria's eyes. She agreed and soon began training for the new job. She answered the phones and helped with some translation when students asked. She learned to operate the printer and to do data entry on the center's computers.

Also, Maria eagerly continued to participate in English conversation groups at the center and became a voracious reader, as if she were making up for lost time. Maria's English fluency continued to impress Sister Ann.

In fact, Maria was asked by Sister Ann if she would be a speaker before a group of nurses at Aurora University. The speakers would be asked what it was like to be a non-English speaking person dealing with medical professionals. Sister Ann invited Maria because she could talk about her first-hand experiences of trying to help her children and herself whenever they saw a doctor.

Maria was thrilled with the invitation, especially since her opinion was valued and her insights could help others understand her experiences. She wanted them to know what it was like to walk into a medical office when they could not speak English and were unable to fully communicate their needs directly to the nurses and doctors unless her husband was there to act as a translator. She wanted to share her experience on what it was like on the other side of their clipboard. She quickly and diligently went to work on her remarks.

When the day arrived, Maria stood with Sister Ann and another speaker before about 25 nurses in the audience, all looking for insights on how to improve their profession and to better help patients. Maria was nervous, but she then grew stronger because she knew what she had to say was important and reached beyond just herself. It was about so many more people like her. And it would enlighten these nurses on the everyday difficulties faced by non-English speaking people when they were trying to acclimate into American society.

Maria talked about her embarrassment whenever she insisted that her husband take time off from work, which caused him to lose wages for the unworked time, just so he could act as a translator at the doctor's office. She especially felt embarrassed when she needed to see a doctor for female-related issues and, again, needed her husband to translate for her. The experience made her feel tied down to a situation that was uncomfortable and made her feel helpless.

Maria was glad those difficult moments were behind her. Since learning English, Maria also learned to drive and get her driver's license, which, in turn, allowed her to feel confident enough to directly help her family. She could go to the doctor by herself, just as a woman, have those appointments in private and freely describe what was necessary so she could be treated or advised. She began learning first-hand how to take care of herself as a woman and as a mother and relished this newly gained freedom.

Maria never realized that something most American women do regularly, and take for granted, she was now able to do after much work and accomplishment. She also never expected to be sharing such private thoughts with a room full of strangers, either. But these strangers were all health care professionals who needed to hear this perspective in order to open their eyes and their hearts to all patients coming through their doors.

At that moment, Sister Ann learned another side of Maria and was very touched by her remarks to the nurses. It showed the difficulties Maria had to overcome in her everyday life. The nurses hung on to her every word.

After her first public speech, Maria continued to study hard and improved herself. In some ways, it also proved to her relatives that she was someone of substance. She accomplished that goal, but still, felt like something was missing in her life. She wasn't done.

"I used to dream that one day I will do something good with my life." Maria told her husband. "I didn't go to college. I didn't have the money. And my father didn't think it was important. So, while I didn't go to college, I feel good that my children could. I am glad I had the strength to pursue my dreams and to keep pushing."

Chapter 24

THE CENTER MARKS ITS 25TH ANNIVERSARY

In 2017, Sister Kathleen set up a committee with tutors and board members to arrange a special event to mark the Dominican Literacy Center's 25th anniversary in Aurora. They targeted October 2018 for the celebration.

Alison Brzezinski, the ESL tutoring coordinator, along with some board members and tutors gathered for several meetings to arrange the anniversary activities and how to solicit donations to support the event. They ultimately garnered two major sponsors and other donors, including Thomas and Ann Sullivan, who were active in their Naperville church's faith sharing group, and Kevin Fitzpatrick, an Aurora businessman.

Food that would be served at the event included tacos, pizza and a celebratory cake. But they planned to ask students and others if they would bring a dish to share on the buffet table. The sharing would enhance their sense of community, which was at the heart of their mission throughout all of these years.

The kids also would enjoy face painting and a large blow-up castle to bounce in. There would be music and dancing. And to highlight memories of the last 25 years, a tent would be erected to house pictures of students, all shown in rotation on a laptop screen.

***

On a cold, foggy day in January 2018, Sister Kathleen started her day with a meeting of students gathering for the first tutoring day after the holidays. She updated them on their English sessions and mentioned the staff was open to suggestions on how to celebrate the center's upcoming 25th anniversary.

They also presented a birthday cake to a student originally from Colombia. The 40-year-old woman smiled at the birthday wishes and said she planned to visit her native country soon. Leftovers were then moved to the kitchen and the cake quickly disappeared. The long wooden table in the adjacent dining room had piles of winter hats, gloves and other donated items, all free to those who needed them.

The meeting broke up and everyone scurried across the two floors and the basement to find their small, individual rooms for the tutoring sessions. About a dozen students were matched to volunteer tutors for one-on-one sessions in the private rooms of the former convent, which at one time had been 10-by-6 bedrooms. The rooms were sparse, but functional. While some rooms had maroon-colored floor tiles, others had green tiles mixed with spots of beige. A white board was on the wall above the table, where the tutor wrote with markers and then used an eraser to clean off the board. Behind them was a small computer desk with an older model PC with a monitor and a steno chair.

Each of the rooms had a single window with a lace curtain and a rod extending just below the top of the wooden frame. A small white clock on the wall, a wooden cabinet near the door and a potted plant decorated the rooms. In the basement, the rooms had cinder block walls with pipes that ran the length of the ceiling and along the baseboards.

The volunteer tutors included some retired teachers, who sat with their student at a small round table in each room. They used workbooks for the lessons and diligently went page by page.

In one room, Sophia and her tutor, Jane, sat next to each other and used the Grammar Work I Book, where she repeated the phrases related to someone's profession. Then Jane pointed to different photos.

"What's this? And this?" Jane asked.

"It's a book. It's a chair," Sophia replied.

The tutor went line by line. "Is this a book? When you make a statement, you say 'It is a book." Jane said, "There is a difference between 'they are,' 'they're' and 'there.' Even Americans get this mixed up."

In a nearby room, another tutor and student worked together. She looked in the book and saw a picture of someone who wanted to dance. The tutor asked her if she liked to dance. She did, but she but didn't think she was very good.

They traded phrases in order to learn: She is beautiful …. boring … disgusting … friendly … funny … intelligent … charming. The tutor explained charming, "as someone who knows all the right things to say."

All of those scenes contrasted sharply from the very first time Sister Kathleen sat down at a table with Juanita, just the two of them, in those early days of the center.

***

As the 25th anniversary celebration approached, Sister Kathleen and her staff ensured that the event would be well organized, vendors would be paid, and an estimate of attendees was tallied.

When October 14, 2018, arrived, Sister Kathleen dressed in layers to fend off the unusually cold day. She wore beige slacks, a turtleneck, and the special-issue T-shirt promoting the center, which read "Empowering our community for 25 years." She then topped it all off with a jacket. She looked at herself in the mirror. She wasn't wearing the black-and-white habit worn by Dominican sisters in the past. She hadn't for decades. She also didn't have this gray hair 25 years ago.

Then again, 25 years ago, she was on the cusp of a new mission, which has since helped thousands of students who sought a dream to blend into American society, to communicate and to live their lives. She and the other sisters and tutors all helped to guide them toward those dreams.

In a way, having the 25th anniversary event outside, in clear public view, turned into an unexpected statement. During the past year, they became worried when the U.S. border with Mexico erupted into turmoil and became a politically hot issue. As parents fled horrible poverty, crime and other circumstances in Ecuador, Guatemala and Honduras, they sought asylum in the United States. Traumatized children were forcibly taken from the arms of their parents, who were asylum seekers and apprehended at the border. They were thrown into metal cages with little food and water and little or no personal care items, like a simple bar of soap.

Other immigrants working in local restaurants were apprehended by U.S. Immigration and Customs Enforcement (ICE). Sister Kathleen also heard about the ICE officers roaming the streets of Aurora and how fearful it made many of her students. She had never asked her students whether they were documented or not. It did not matter to their mission of teaching English.

But she wondered what the future would be like for

these young families arriving to a country once known for its American dream. Yes, the 25th anniversary celebration was being held outside because of the hundreds of expected guests. In a way, it also would show the public that these immigrants came in peace to assimilate into a new society and to contribute to that society.

Now, the adrenaline of this 25th anniversary celebration shifted into high gear as Sister Kathleen worked with others to set up tables on the grounds around the center. She wanted to ensure that everything was in place and that guests would have a good time, regardless of the cool weather. She even directed some staff to set up some heaters around the perimeter.

Nearly 450 people arrived throughout the afternoon, all wearing jackets. But the cool breezes didn't stop their enthusiasm. Many former students reunited with their former tutors to catch up or reminisce, while children played, and music tied the whole event together.

After many ate tacos, pizza, popcorn and other foods shared on a buffet table, Sister Kathleen gathered the speakers to address the crowd. One of the speakers was U.S. Representative Bill Foster, a tall, slender businessman-turned-physicist-turned-government leader and a Democrat, representing the 11th District that includes Aurora. Sister Kathleen spotted Congressman Foster, with his thinning gray hair, glasses, blue suit and red tie. She waved him over.

The congressman walked over and stood next to Sister Kathleen and thanked her for establishing the center. He then presented to her a page of the U.S. Congressional Record inside a decorative folder. He read it aloud to the crowd:

"Mr. Speaker, I rise today to recognize the Dominican Literacy Center's 25th anniversary.

Since 1993, the Dominican Literacy Center has helped over 2,500 women learn to read, write and speak English. Through individual tutoring by trained volunteers, this trusted organization has assisted hardworking individuals in becoming active members of the community. These services are incredibly important for cities like Aurora, where 42 percent of residents are immigrants from other countries and speak English as a second language.

"I would like to thank the Dominican Literacy Center for its commitment to the citizens of Illinois and for its contributions to the Aurora, Illinois community."

The crowd applauded. Sister Kathleen smiled and thanked the congressman and all the students and families who braved the cold weather to celebrate with them. To hear that number — 2,500 — seemed magical. It was a number Sister Kathleen never thought the center would reach 25 years ago, especially when it started in the basement of a church, where old tables and chairs were used for those early tutoring sessions.

The literacy center eventually went from a basement to a

larger building and helped to launch a second center. The Aurora center started with $20,000 in grants and grew to an annual budget of about $235,000 to support a small staff and fund future growth.

That year, the Aurora center had 183 volunteer tutors serving 204 students while the Melrose Park center had 32 tutors serving 80 students. More students were on waiting lists. And when students finished the English program, they often signed up for classes to prepare for the U.S. citizenship test held at St. Mary's Parish on Downer Place in Aurora. The expansion of the center's services helped these students reach their potential.

After the congressman spoke, Sister Kathleen turned to Juany Garza, an alderwoman with the city of Aurora who oversaw the district where the center is based. When Juany left Mexico and arrived in the United States in 1972, she did not know English, just like many of the former students standing before her in the growing crowd.

Juany felt like she knew each of these women. She knew the Latino community in Aurora and felt the literacy center was especially important to the Latinas. It helped them to learn the language so they could find jobs and become more independent.

She held her head high when she began to speak.

"When I first had my daughter, I went to the hospital here and I couldn't even say I wanted a cup of coffee with cream and sugar," Garza said. "I learned English from my daughter when she went to school. They also didn't have Spanish on the menus in restaurants or on TV or on the radio back then. We had to learn English, in order to do more with our lives. So, the opportunity you had to go to this center, to learn English, to learn the language, that is what makes you stronger. Many of you went on to get good jobs, some even got great jobs. You went to work in offices. Or you owned a business. You were very happy to make something more of yourself, especially the women. Congratulations to the center on its 25th anniversary."

In the back of the crowd, Juanita Rodriguez beamed.

Juanita was like so many others who followed the center and the career of Sister Kathleen over the years. It was because she helped people like Juanita, who were stuck between two worlds, searching for their path. She was among the women who also inspired Sister Kathleen to persevere with the center for 25 years, despite an economic downturn and tumultuous political times. Eventually, they actually learned from each other and both Sister Kathleen and her students found their paths.

"She is special," Juanita said to the lady next to her in the crowd. "We are very proud of Sister Kathleen. She was always so very busy, but when you asked her things, she would take the time to listen to you."

Juanita's daughter, Vanessa, became a member of the

center's board and was volunteering at the 25th anniversary celebration. She wouldn't miss it. She helped to serve food and volunteered for the activities. Vanessa's action showed how much she appreciated what the center did for her mother and others like her.

Sister Kathleen scanned the hundreds of people around her. It took her breath away. She saw the face of God in each of them.

Twenty-five years ago, there was just a handful of students. None of them had any expectations that it would be this successful or even last this long. Over the years, those 2,500 students arrived through the center's front doors from about 30 different countries. They all left behind their relatives, friends and homes in Mexico, Venezuela, Argentina, Peru, Colombia, Honduras, Cameroon, Myanmar, Iraq, China, Dominican Republic, Cuba, Ecuador, Russia, South Korea and elsewhere. They were women who were determined to learn and to adapt.

They were part of a melting pot, and today, they all were enjoying each other's company, all remembering what they were like years ago compared to now. Sister Kathleen remembered how students depended on books and magazines to explain English words. Now, the majority use mobile phones with all the computer resources resting in the palm of their hand.

Sister Kathleen always asked students if they grasped the

meaning of words or if they needed more time with a tutor. She just never asked if they came into the country legally or not. After 25 years, it still was not relevant to the center's mission.

That strategy proved successful at the Dominican Literacy Center. Every day the volunteers worked with immigrant women, who were discouraged or fearful because they lacked skills in English. But these women found refuge at the center because they were welcomed with a smile and a helping hand. It nourished their goals of assimilating into a new culture and a chance at the American dream.

It was those earlier students that Sister Kathleen remembered the most on this milestone anniversary — the ones from poor towns in Mexico who created an urgent need for the literacy centers. English helped break the cycle of illiteracy for these women and opened new doors for them, both in society and in their personal lives. As Sister Kathleen stood there, she reflected on the stories of these determined women.

Sister Kathleen smiled at Juanita, who stood in the distance holding a bouquet of flowers. Juanita had escaped poverty in Guanajuato, Mexico and the men who threatened to rape her. Since she learned English at the center, Juanita and her husband, Jaime, were proud to raise their children, who later were the first to attend college. Vanessa was in college, while Yesenia became a nurse practitioner. Andy was going to NIU and worked as a personal trainer and firefighter. Their daughters also married and began families without the fear of poverty that their parents faced.

Juanita also enjoyed being a babysitter for her four grandchildren, helping her daughters to avoid the expense of childcare. It also gave her time to be with her grandchildren and to watch them with the experience she learned while raising her own children. Most of all, she talked with them in English and it helped them to bond. Learning English also helped to fulfill her dreams as she became part of the lives of the next generation.

Then there was Blanca Gonzales Aguilera, a housekeeper at a medical office, who was determined to fulfill her dreams in America by learning English. She earned a GED, became a U.S. citizen, earned promotions to become a supervisor at work and contributed for more than 20 years with a successful career, all while raising a family and dealing with health issues. She also proved to her children that education never ends and it should always be a part of their lives. That attitude helped her to learn English at the center, which opened new doors for herself and her family with her job promotion. That's what Blanca continued to instill in her children. She asked each of them to go to school, to work hard and to get what she did not get: a college degree.

Blanca's oldest daughter, Diana, earned a bachelor of science degree in health information management at the

University of Illinois at Chicago. Another daughter, Rocio, earned a bachelor of science degree in operations management and information systems and a master of science degree in management information systems, both at NIU. She later landed a job as product owner/digital experience at the cosmetic retail chain, Ulta Beauty Inc. in Bolingbrook, Illinois. Blanca's son, Ricardo, earned a bachelor of arts degree in Spanish at NIU and became an assistant director of transfer admission and bilingual outreach at Dominican University in River Forest, Illinois. Blanca beamed with pride every time she saw her children and she shed tears of joy as they became part of the first generation in their family to graduate from college.

In some ways, Blanca felt just as proud of herself because she had the initiative to move to a foreign country, to learn the English language and to pursue her dreams. She learned to drive, got a license and earned a GED, all while raising a family. She also learned about the American way of life, and she and Eusebio saved enough money to own their own home. She tried to instill similar values in her children and urged them to get a job and save their money. Most of all, they needed to be careful how they spent that money.

While she endured back-breaking laborious work, made many sacrifices to raise her family, and spent years learning English, Blanca felt it was all worth it. Blanca's philosophy was always to be happy. And when she dies, she told her family, she wants it to be a happy time. No tears. No sadness. She wants only happiness because she lived and helped her family. She wants just to live in peace and know that when her time comes, she can say goodbye with peace.

The largest life lesson Blanca learned was to be grateful and to give praise and honor to God. It was only through God's love, mercy, graciousness and endless blessings that she overcame the obstacles in her life. There were many points in her journey when she did not know if she would ever marry, be able to find work or even keep the house that she and her husband had bought. But through constant and fervent prayer, they met those challenges and overcame any problems. For Blanca, it was only through God that she had what she considered to be the best life ever imagined. And only because of Him, she continued to live a life she thought she could only dream about.

"I never look back. I always look forward," said Blanca. "Most of my dreams, if not all of my dreams, were here in the United States. I got more than I deserved. I do not need anything else. I pray a lot. And always, God is first."

Then there was Teresa Trenado, who escaped laboring in fields, married a farm hand and later lived through a massive earthquake and gas explosions in Mexico City. She then moved to the United States, raised a family, learned English and fulfilled her dream of attaining U.S. citizenship. Since then, Teresa gained confidence in her language and her actions. She also gained more pride after watching her children graduate from high school, find good jobs and begin married lives. Eventually, seven grandchildren would come along.

When Teresa and Miguel started out as newlyweds in Mexico, they didn't have anything. Now, they have many blessings, including the extra money to make return visits to Mexico to see their relatives. Teresa's first trip back brought tears to her eyes when she saw her old home, now empty since both of her parents have passed away. Despite the hardships and losses, Teresa felt she had gained much. Also, her son, Lazaro, did not forget the donated toys he received from the sisters at the Dominican Literacy Center. Years later, Lazaro gathered some friends and they drove carloads of donated toys to the center. He presented the toys to Sister Kathleen, so other young children also could enjoy their Christmas holiday.

Then there was Maria Dominguez, who washed the family's clothes on a rock in a stream by their home in Valle de Juarez, Mexico, until she shed her fears and went to America. After she learned English, she got a driver's license, gained enough confidence to take care of her children without a translator and became a U.S. citizen.

Maria's daughter, Paola, and her sons, Mauricio and Alonzo, were the first generation in their family to earn college degrees. Paola earned a bachelor's degree and, later, a master's degree at NIU. She became a kindergarten teacher, married and had two children. Mauricio earned a psychology degree from the University of Illinois at Champaign finishing in the top 3% of his class and found a job with a non-profit. Alonzo graduated with a bachelor's degree in computer science at Western Illinois University in Macomb and later joined the U.S. Army doing computer work. Maria knew that if she had not left Mexico, her children may never have attended college.

Sister Kathleen also remembered Maribel Molina Cortes, who escaped brutal beatings from an abusive husband, fended off starvation and supported herself and her daughter by cleaning toilets. After learning English, she found better-paying jobs and a promotion, opened her first savings account, bought her first home, and eventually opened and operated her own restaurant. She later trained for and ran in the Chicago Marathon.

To thank God, Maribel then donated new clothes to adults and school supplies and treats to needy children in Tlaxcala, Mexico. She also became a permanent resident of the United States and was on the path to becoming a U.S. citizen.

Many more women who followed these early students also attended the celebration. They all learned English from the Dominican Sisters and volunteer tutors. Over the years, many of them also advanced toward U.S. citizenship. They got better jobs and promotions, fed their families, paid their bills and saved to buy their first homes. They later saw their children as the first generation to graduate high school and college, instead of working in the fields or factories or cleaning someone else's toilet or washing clothes on a rock.

These proud immigrant women now were facing retirement and babysitting grandchildren, the next generation that reflected their hopes for the future in the United States.

Sister Kathleen witnessed, as the other tutors have, that each of these immigrants believed enough in themselves and their families to boot-strap their lives. They raised their families and worked hard to prove their self-worth was part of a mighty path to more chances in life. They also discovered that reliance that grew deep within themselves also mirrored their tenacity and spirit, just as much as the Dominican Sisters used that same reserve to pray and to listen to the Lord.

And it all started with Juanita as the first student. Juanita was proud of that. The center helped to change her life — and many other lives — forever.

Juanita nodded when she caught Sister Kathleen's eye after the speeches. She walked up to Sister Kathleen and they embraced. Juanita then handed the bouquet of flowers to Sister Kathleen.

"Thank you so much," Juanita said. "I love you!"

"I love you, too," Sister Kathleen said.

ACKNOWLEDGMENTS

I am deeply indebted to an array of talented, dedicated people who helped me as I wrote this book. A heartfelt thank you goes to:

The Dominican Sisters of Springfield, Illinois, especially Sisters Beth Murphy, Kathleen Ryan, Ann Clennon, Judith Curran and Beverly Jeanne Howe for sharing their experiences and insights.

Maribel Molina Cortes, Juanita Rodriguez, Maria Dominguez, Blanca Aguilera and Teresa Trenado, who courageously left behind the only worlds they knew so they could start new lives in the United States.

Kathie Walsh, who represents what many tutors have experienced when starting a new journey to help others.

Patrick M. Kinnally for his time and expertise regarding the law, immigration and education.

Deacon David Brencic, my former newspaper colleague and long-time friend; Katherine Kaloydis Obmascik, a freelance writer and editor; and Maria Arza, a former co-worker, who each provided editing guidance and suggestions to help point this book in the right direction.

Jackie Camacho-Ruiz, Michele Kelly and the Fig Factor Media staff for their direction and encouragement throughout the publishing process.

Most of all, Jim Tomczyk, my wonderful husband, who provided loving advice, steadfast support and valuable insights. He always encouraged me to soar like an eagle to accomplish my dreams.

ABOUT THE AUTHOR

Anna Marie Kukec Tomczyk is a Chicago-based, award-winning journalist and writer. She wrote under her maiden name of Anna Marie Kukec for U.S. News & World Report, ABA Journal, Chicago Tribune, Chicago Sun-Times, Daily Herald, Prepared Foods Magazine, Chicago Bride Magazine and others.

She began as a reporter, columnist and section editor at the Daily Southtown, where she covered Chicago's south suburbs and interviewed myriad TV and film celebrities. She earned various awards from the former Suburban Press Club of Chicago for her Spotlight on Youth column and stories about a community college professor charged with espionage in the former Yugoslavia. She also received various honors, including Woman of the Year from Evergreen Park High School, her alma mater.

Anna Marie then learned to work on both sides of the aisle as a speechwriter and spokeswoman for the Illinois Attorney General's Office, serving both Democrat and Republican administrations, and was one of the spokespeople during the execution of mass murderer, John Wayne Gacy, and other cases. In addition, she volunteered in similar roles for two gubernatorial campaigns. Next, she became a reporter for the American Bar Association's Bar Leader Magazine, covering bar associations and legal cases nationwide.

Afterward, Anna Marie worked as a senior writer at the Daily Herald and its Business Ledger Magazine in Arlington Heights, Illinois, where she interviewed CEOs of Fortune 500 companies and questioned President George W. Bush during a nationally televised press conference. During this time, she won a Chicago Headline Club Lisagor Award as part of a team reporting on the Illinois minimum wage. She also was the lead writer and coordinator of the four-part series, "The Dream Foreclosed," about residential foreclosures that earned first-place awards in public service from the Illinois Associated Press Editors Association, the Chicago Journalists Association's Sarah Brown Boyden Award, the National Federation of Press Women, the Illinois Woman's Press Association as well as the Chicago Bar Association's Herman Kogan Awards Meritorious Achievement. She also earned a first-place award in business reporting from the Northern Illinois Newspaper Association for a story about the impact of an acquisition on a small company. In addition, she was an occasional guest on ABC7-TV, WBBM Radio and WGN Radio news shows in Chicago.

In 2017, she decided to leave the Daily Herald to do contract writing for various nationwide publications and the U.S. Department of Energy's Argonne National Laboratory. In 2020, she founded the book-writing company, Forest Glen Media LLC.

Anna Marie is a member of the Chicago Writers Association, Independent Writers of Chicago, the Society of Professional Journalists and the Chicago Headline Club.

She is a graduate of St. Xavier University in Chicago, where she lives with her husband, Jim Tomczyk, a project manager and a lifelong Chicago Bears fan.

Connect with her on LinkedIn, Facebook, Instagram and as @AMKukec on Twitter.

FOR MORE INFORMATION

Dominican Literacy Center

Sister Kathleen Ryan, O.P., Administrator

Email: domlitctr@sbcglobal.net

260 Vermont Avenue

Aurora, Illinois 60505

Phone: (630) 898-4636

Website: https://dominicanliteracycenter.org

Donations:https://www.mightycause.com/organization/
Dominican-Literacy-Center-Aurora

Dominican Literacy Center

Sister Judith Curran, O.P., Administrator

1503 Rice Street

Melrose Park, Illinois 60160

Phone: (708) 338-0659

Dominican Sisters of Springfield

Sister Beth Murphy, O.P., Director of Communications

Email: SBMurphy@spdom.org

Sister Kathleen Anne Tait, O.P., Director of Donations

Email: skatait@spdom.org

1237 W. Monroe

Springfield, Illinois 62704

Phone: (217) 787-0481

Website: https://springfieldop.org

Donations: https://interland3.donorperfect.net/weblink/
weblink.aspx?name=E229831&id=14

*A portion of the profits from this book will be donated to the
Dominican Literacy Center.*